Burkard Polster is Senior Lecturer in Pure Mathematics at Monash University in Australia. An established ambigram artist he is the author of numerous scholarly works as well as *The Shoelace Book: A Mathematical Guide to the Best (and Worst) Ways to Lace Your Shoes*, *The Mathematics of Juggling* and *Q.E.D.: Beauty in Mathematical Proof*. He is also a magician, juggler, origami expert, bubble-master and shoelace charmer.

Burkard Polster

Eye Twisters

Ambigrams & Other Visual Puzzles to Amaze and Entertain

STERLING
New York / London
www.sterlingpublishing.com

10 9 8 7 6 5 4 3 2 1

First published in 2008 by Sterling Publishing Co., Inc.
387 Park Avenue South, New York, NY 10016

Distributed in Canada by Sterling Publishing
c/o Canadian Manda Group, 165 Dufferin Street
Toronto, Ontario, Canada M6K 3H6

For information about custom editions, special sales, premium and corporate purchases, please contact Sterling Special Sales Department at 800-805-5489 or specialsales@sterlingpub.com.

Sterling ISBN-13: 978-1-4027-5798-3
ISBN-10: 1-4027-5798-0

Printed and bound in China

CONTENTS

Just Imagine

Foreword by John Langdon

Imagine a world in which the spaces between things are also things – as if there are no spaces. A world in which things turned upside-down are still right-side-up. A world in which the laws of nature as we know them can be suspended or ignored – or perhaps expanded – at least for the time being.

Some of us do imagine what might come next. We see the world around us, and out of the awe and love inspired by that world we imagine things that are not there – or perhaps they are there, but most people seem not to see them. It's as if the world around us gets our minds racing with such joy that we forget to stop, where most people, seeing that the pavement ends, stop and turn around. But rather than hurtle headlong into the underbrush, we take flight.

I cannot write this foreword as an outside observer. Among my various job descriptions is 'ambigram artist'. Along with Scott Kim, Peter Jones and Douglas Hofstadter, I pioneered the phenomenon of ambigrams. Nevertheless, we were not the first to imagine language that could take on not only visual significance, but symbolism that transcends imagery and reaches into metaphysical realms. There are numerous examples of such phenomena throughout history, including spiritual interpretations of the shapes of letters in certain alphabets. Ambigrams specifically – though unnamed as such – have been around for at least a hundred years. Within the limits of my own knowledge, they were regarded primarily as curious amusements – parlour tricks. They were ahead of their time and, as is often the case with such things, they attracted little notice. But ambigrams are now of their time, and this book appropriately celebrates ambigrams, as well as their numerous non-verbal cousins – an extended family of visual astonishments that delight the eye and mind, and point the way into imaginary worlds – or real worlds that only quantum physicists and mystics have been familiar with to date.

But it is not only science's intrepid journeys into fantastic realms that establish the relevance of the wonderful realities these works of art reveal. The world having been shrunk not only by the previous century's advances in transportation and communication, but also by the more contemporary phenomenon of the worldwide web, there has never been a greater need for human beings to entertain the notion of looking at things from vantage points beyond those provided by our provincial cultural heritages and our own limited experiences. The stubborn adherence to 'realities' created by those forces has led to poverty, discrimination, intolerance and war. If we are to survive as a species, we will need to give credence to and seek understanding of the realities experienced by human beings in other cultures – indeed, other species as well – with other points of view. It may seem a quantum leap from ambigrams and ambiguous images to saving ourselves and our planet from colossal catastrophes of our own making, but perhaps through art, the resistance to other points of view can be eroded.

Burkard Polster, in addition to being a mathematician, is an ambigram artist. And it is by way of ambigrams that he has created *Eye Twisters*. But for all their visual appeal and intellectual stimulation, ambigrams lack the ability to communicate in the way that pictorial images can. And Burkard has, therefore, balanced those gymnastic and contortionist words with graphics and illustrations that expand the viewer's mind towards similar destinations, but by different paths. For most of us – ambigram and non-ambigram artists alike – Maurits Cornelis Escher was perhaps our most important inspiration. We are all indebted to him, and homages to him abound in this book. But it was Dan Brown who seared ambigrams into the imaginations of millions of readers around the world, at the same time as they were seared into the chests of murdered ecclesiastical leaders of the Catholic Church in his novel *Angels & Demons.*

Scott Kim, Douglas Hofstadter and I have all written books about our own individual work in the esoteric field of ambigrams. You hold in your hand the first book that brings together the work of many prominent ambigram artists and creators of outstanding pictorial optical illusions. *Eye Twisters* not only catalogues the verbal and visual ambiguous images that helped create this wonderland, but also reveals recent expansions of the art of ambigrams, well beyond the symmetry and reversibility of single words and the occasional short phrase. From my point of view, the most exciting new work in this field involves pushing ambigrams into further dimensions – sometimes in actual 3-D, sometimes virtual. Tom Banwell has taken what has been largely a two-dimensional art into tangible, three-dimensional sculptures. Several of Patrice Hamel's ambigrams involve projected and/or reflected light. Burkard Polster has harnessed the capabilities of software programs with which he creates exciting multi-faceted images that imply dimensions un- or under-explored by previous ambigrammists. Yet my favourite of all of Burkard's work is the photographic image of his daughter, Lara, both gripping and in the grip of an almost dizzying spiral reality.

The time for this book has arrived. The time for you to turn its pages has arrived. Where will *Eye Twisters* take you?

Just imagine.

word

ambigram

play

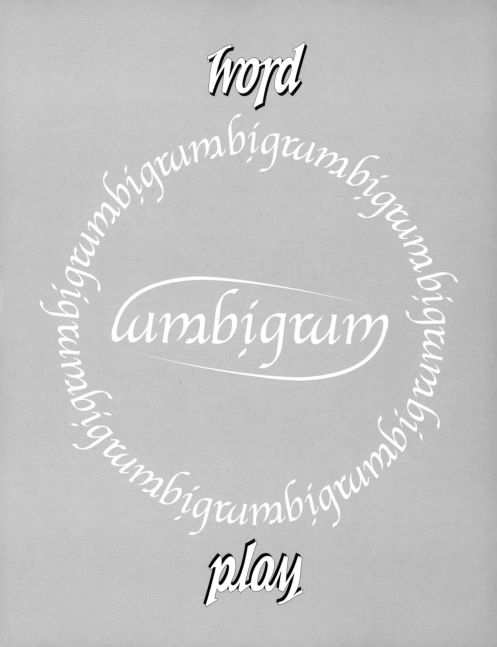

What on Earth is an Ambigram?

Before you read on, have a really close look at the following word. It looks pretty, but can you spot anything else that is special about it?

If your answer is 'No', then prepare to be amazed: turn this book upside-down and look at the word again. Unlike any ordinary way of writing *wordplay*, this calligraphic version stays unchanged when you give it a spin. This is a beautiful example of an ambigram, a calligraphic design that has not just one but two interpretations as a written word. Maybe those who answered 'No' to my question would have been even more surprised if I had shown them just the first half of this ambigram, because when you turn it upside-down it turns into a *different* word. This means that the first half, and therefore the second half, are ambigrams in their own right.

Although ambigrams have been around for a long time, not many people were aware of their existence. This changed only recently after millions of people discovered some superb examples by ambigram master John

Langdon in Dan Brown's bestselling novel *Angels & Demons*. The *wordplay* ambigram above is also by John Langdon.

As a consequence, the world seems to have gone ambigram crazy – many people have started making ambigrams of their own, others are having ambigram tattoos etched into their skin, and even the fact that you are holding this book in your hands is due to the current interest in ambigrams. The word 'ambigram' is still not an official Scrabble word at the time of writing this book and the compilers of dictionaries don't seem to know about it, but this is bound to change.

There are few people who are not intrigued by ambigrams, but as with magic tricks, there are different levels of appreciation: you may just be happy to watch the trick performed and be enchanted by it, you may feel compelled to 'figure it out', you may want to master it yourself, or you may want to go on and invent your own magic tricks. Here are only a few examples of the many reasons why some people are driven to go beyond the first level of appreciation in the case of ambigrams.

Ambigrams are the kind of trickery that the famous Dutch artist M. C. Escher would have engaged in, had he known about them. Just like Escher's amazing mosaics with animals, ambigrams combine geometrical symmetries with real-life objects. They exhibit both mathematical and natural beauty, a combination that those with a scientific mind find irresistible. Unlike with Escher's drawings, it is fairly easy to make the transition from looking at ambigrams to creating your own.

Douglas Hofstadter, the author of the Pulitzer Prize-winning book *Gödel, Escher, Bach,* is a professor of cognitive science who also coined the word 'ambigram'. For him ambigrams form an ideal microworld for the study of creativity. Over the years he has created thousands of ambigrams and observed other ambigram artists in an effort to unravel some of the mysteries of creativity.

To typography and logo specialists, ambigrams present one of the ultimate technical challenges. How do you twist and turn letters into calligraphic masterpieces that can be read naturally in two different ways and spell out the same or different messages? Have another look at the *wordplay* ambigram. If you had encountered it outside the context of this book, would you have ever suspected that there was more to it than meets the eye at first glance?

The ambigrams of masters like John Langdon present a new form of poetry in which ordinary words turn into magic spells of real power and new meaning.

On a more personal note, I thought it would be a romantic idea to create one ambigram present a day for the girl of my dreams for as long as it took to win her over. An ambigram of her name, an ambigram that fused both our names, and so on. And it actually worked for me! It took about thirty such presents, but in the end she married me.

Ambigram Spotting

You may have noticed that NO turns into ON when you turn it upside-down and that NOON stays unchanged. Or perhaps you have even come across the famous swimming pool sign: NOW NO SWIMS ON MON which makes sure that even those people who are in the habit of walking around on their hands won't have any problems figuring out that the pool is closed on Mondays.

What other *natural* ambigrams like these are there? Well, that depends a little bit on what you think of as 'natural' and what words are permitted. I did a little bit of a computer search and the list on the right is what I came up with. This list is rather short, but contains a few other interesting natural ambigrams. I recommend using MOM turning into WOW on a birthday card for your mother.

ale
axe
suns
seas
sales
solos
newsman

we am
aid pie
new man
sine anis

OH HO
ON NO
NIM WIN
OHM WHO
NOW MON
WOW MOM
SNOW MONS

VIA
SOS
OHO
NON
MOW
NOON
SWIMS

The French fashion label *NEW MAN* uses the natural ambigram pair in its logo, and I always wondered whether the name of the game NIM came about by turning the word WIN upside-down.

NEW MAN

Who Invented Ambigrams?

People must have been aware of natural ambigrams for a very long time, and many people must have played with upside-down words. This makes it hard to pinpoint exactly who *invented* ambigrams. Was it the first person who noticed that NOON stays unchanged when you turn it upside-down, or was it the first person who created an 'unnatural' ambigram? In either case, there is no way of knowing who that person was.

The earliest example of a non-trivial ambigram that I am aware of is the half-turn ambigram in Peter Newel's book of upside-down pictures and stories entitled *Topsys and Turvys – Number 2* which was published in 1902. It reads *puzzle 2* the right side up and *the end* upside-down.

Further early examples include half-turn ambigrams of the words *chump, honey* and the signature of the cartoonist *W. H. Hill*. These ambigrams were published in the British monthly *The Strand* in 1908.

This vintage upside-down picture by Gustave Verbeek works in the same way as all these ambigrams – it shows a hyena eating a bird the right side up and a really big bird devouring a hyena upside-down. Upside-down pictures like this are far more common than their ambigram relatives and the earliest known examples date back a couple of hundred years.

So we do know that there were some people who created some real ambigrams at the beginning of the twentieth century. However, up until quite recently there was not much more than a handful of real ambigrams floating around – hardly enough to warrant a special term to describe them.

From the early 1970s, two young artists, Scott Kim and John Langdon, rediscovered ambigrams independently from each other and anybody else, and started creating professionally crafted ambigrams. Through them a number of other artists became interested in doing the same – in particular, Robert Petrick through his friend and colleague John Langdon, and Douglas Hofstadter through Scott Kim. Quite a few of their ambigrams were published in Scott Morris's column in *Omni* magazine and Martin Gardner's column in *Scientific American*. Four books have been published on ambigrams, by far the most influential of which are Scott Kim's book *Inversions* which appeared in 1981 and John Langdon's book *Wordplay* which was first published in 1992, with a second edition in 2005. Douglas Hofstadter's book *Ambigrammi* appeared in 1987 in Italian and my little book *Ambigrammes* in 2004 in French. Despite all this publicity, for some mysterious reason, ambigrams never became popular until John Langdon's ambigrams made their way into Dan Brown's novel *Angels & Demons*. Even today, Scott and John, who started it all, are the world's most influential ambigram artists.

If you are interested in finding out more about the ambigram artists mentioned above and many others, turn to the chapter *Meet the Artists*. For a very detailed account of the history of ambigrams, have a look at the relevant chapter in John Langdon's book.

Wordplay, the title of John Langdon's 1992 book on ambigrams.

Inversions by Scott Kim: the 1981 book and its author fused into a half-turn ambigram – turn it upside-down and it reads Scott Kim!

Robert Petrick's logo created for the rock band *Angel* in 1975.

Mirror Mirror on the Wall

So far we've seen only one type of ambigram, the so-called half-turn ambigram. However there are many other interesting types. The ambigram *Starship*, created for the rock band of the same name, was one of John Langdon's earliest ambigrams, created around 1973. It is a good example of a *wall-reflection ambigram*. To see the second reading of a wall-reflection ambigram, either hold the ambigram up so it is facing a mirror (e.g. your Mirror on the Wall) or turn over the page it is printed on and hold it against the light. Of course, in the case of John's ambigram, the second reading is also *Starship*. This means that unlike your ordinary word, this ambigram is its own mirror image and if you write it on a piece of glass, it reads the same from both sides.

The special properties of wall-reflection ambigrams make them ideal candidates for some neat real-world applications. Here are just two examples.

Question: Why do they print the word AMBULANCE in mirror writing on ambulances? **Answer:** Because they want to make absolutely sure that you can read the word in your rear mirror when the ambulance is racing towards you from behind. So, wouldn't it be great to have a wall-reflection ambigram of the word ambulance? It would read the right way both when you look at it in a mirror and also when you look at the ambulance straight on. You can admire my best (unsuccessful)

attempt (see above) from a decade ago which, should it ever be used, would probably result in more casualties than it would help prevent. So here is a challenge for you: can you come up with an *ambulance* wall-reflection ambigram that really works? If you do, please let me know.

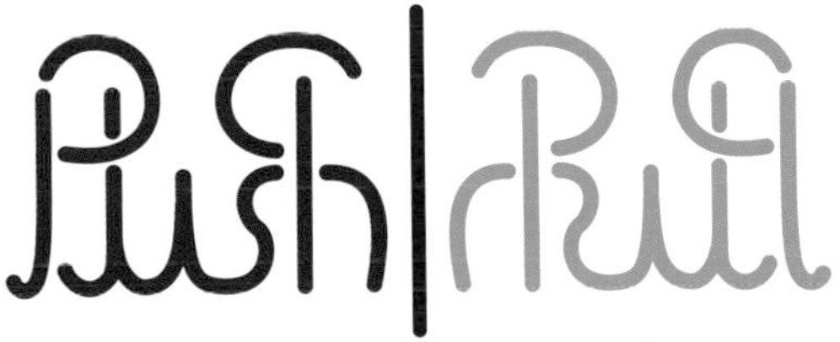

Here is one more challenge. First, imagine the following scenario: hurrying somewhere, a stereotypical mathematician like myself approaches a glass door, absentmindedly reads a 'Push' sign, and a moment later crashes into an unyielding door. What happened? Your favourite mathematician made the mistake of subconsciously deciphering a half-transparent sign that was printed on the other side of the door whose message was meant for people approaching from that side. By replacing the sign by a wall-reflection ambigram that reads *Push* from one side of the door and *Pull* from the other side, perhaps we would save innumerable glass doors. Again, my best attempt from a couple of years ago leaves much to be desired. However, it is probably unreadable enough to slow you down enough to prevent you from crashing into the door. Can anybody do better than this?

Other Geometrical Ambigrams

Half-turn ambigrams and wall-reflection ambigrams are geometrical ambigrams since they are based on geometrical symmetries. The so-called *lake-reflection ambigrams* and *quarter-turn ambigrams* are two more popular types of geometrical ambigrams. Have a look at the examples on this and the following page.

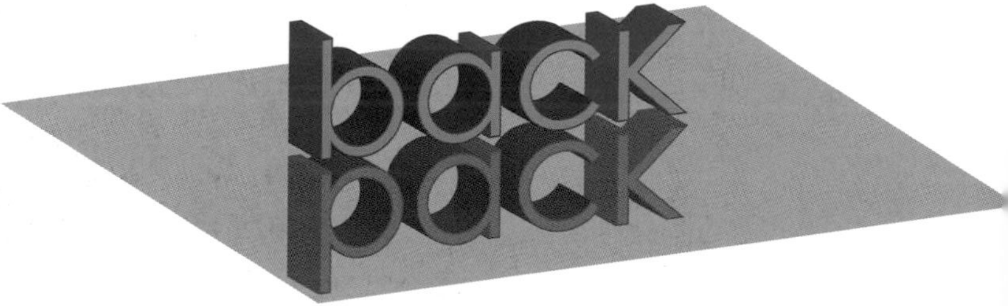

You can see the second reading of a lake-reflection ambigram by looking at its reflection in a horizontal mirror. The word *back* written as shown here is a lake-reflection ambigram that occurs 'in the wild'. Its second reading is *pack*.

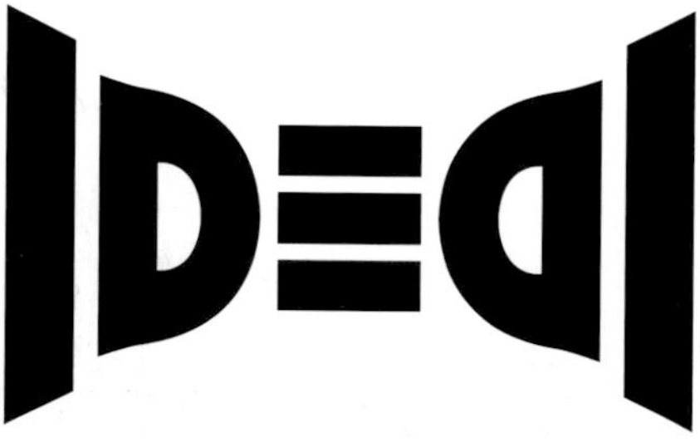

This amazing ambigram of the word *ideal* is by Robert Petrick. It is at the same time a wall-reflection, lake-reflection and half-turn ambigram – it stays unchanged when you look at it in a vertical mirror, when you look at it in a horizontal mirror and when you rotate it 180 degrees.

Two quarter-turn ambigrams by Douglas Hofstadter. Here the name of the famous composer *Bach* turns into *Fuga*, which is the word for *Fugue* in Latin, Italian and Spanish.

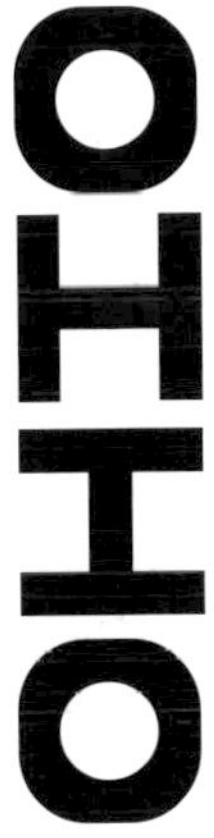

Just like the *ideal* on the left, the word *mom* written in capital letters is at the same time a wall-reflection, lake-reflection and half-turn ambigram. Its second reading is *wow*.

AIM HAT HIT HOT OHM WHO

MOA MIX TAU TAO VIA VOX

ATOM HOAX MATH MOTH VITA YOYO

MOUTH TOOTH VOMIT WITHY WITTY YOUTH

AUTOMAT MAMMOTH MAXIMUM TAXIWAY WITHOUT TIMOTHY

The upper-case letters

AHIMOTUVWXY

all are their own wall reflections. This means that any word made up of these letters, written from top to bottom, is a wall-reflection ambigram. Take a look at this list in a mirror mounted on a wall.

BEE
BIB
BID
DIE
EBB
HOE
ICE
KID
ODD
ODE

BIKE
BOOK
CHIC
COCO
CODE
DECK
DICE
ECHO
HOBO
HOOD
HOOK
KICK
OBOE

BEECH
CHECK
CHICK
COOEE
DIODE
OXIDE

BODICE
BOOKIE
CHOICE
COOKIE
DECIDE
DECODE
EXCEED
ICEBOX
IODIDE
KIDDIE
DIOXIDE

The upper-case letters **BCDEHIKOX** all are their own lake reflections. This means that any word which consists of these letters is a lake-reflection ambigram. Try this: create a 'lake' on your desk by placing a mirror on it. Now, stand the book upright on the mirror and look at this list in the mirror.

Three words that are at the same time wall-reflection, lake-reflection and half-turn ambigrams.

O++O, +OO+, OHO

A magical vortex in which the natural ambigram pair NO-ON performs a very special kind of dance.

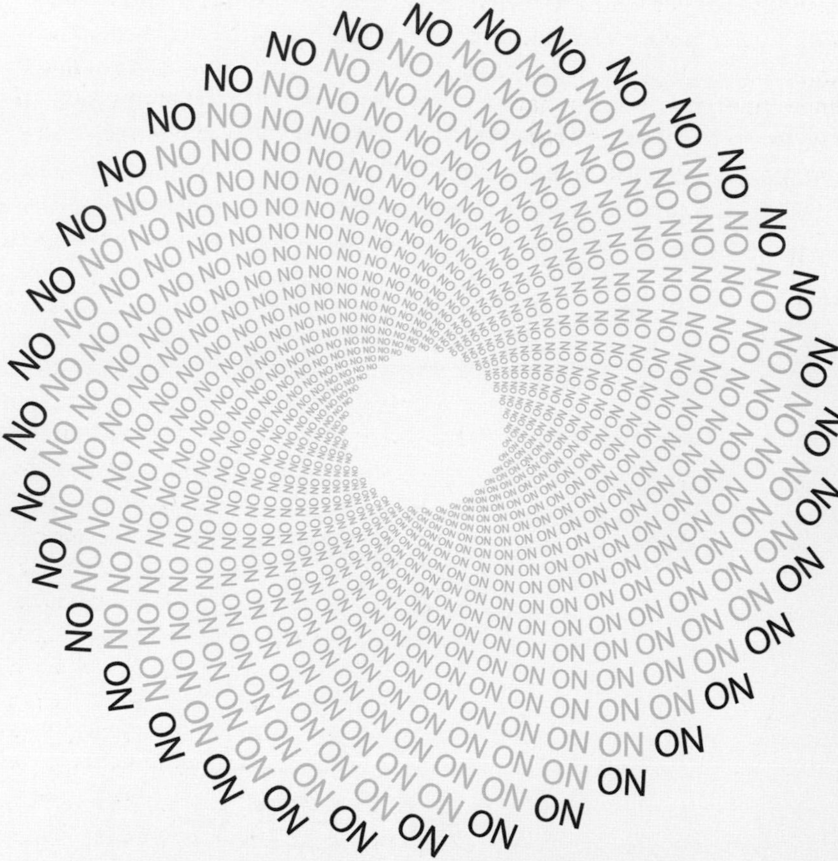

NOON

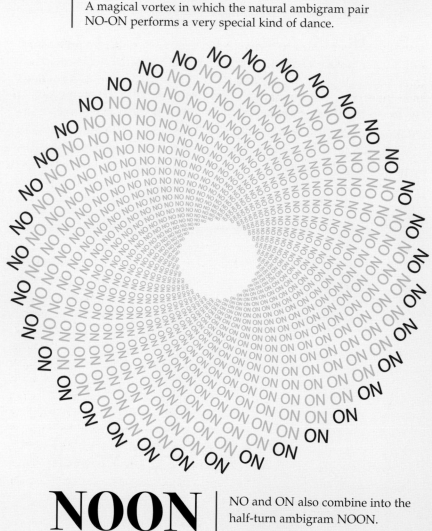

NO and ON also combine into the half-turn ambigram NOON.

Standard, Chain & Ring Ambigrams

Usually it is very hard to turn a given word into a 'good' ambigram of one of the types described above. For example, there is no obvious good way to turn the word *twisters* into a standard-type ambigram. On the other hand, it is not hard to come up with half-turn ambigrams of the two partial words *twist* and *ers*. Using these two ambigrams we can produce a half-turn 'chain' ambigram of twisters as follows.

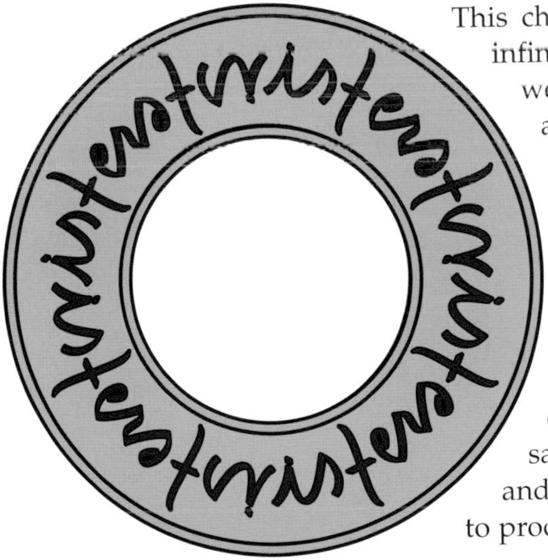

This chain is supposed to continue to infinity on both sides. Alternatively, we can produce a half-turn 'ring' ambigram as shown below which can be read in both the clockwise and counter-clockwise directions. If you succeed in producing a standard-type ambigram of a word, then you can always string multiple copies of this ambigram together to form a chain or ring ambigram of the same type. As a general rule, chain and ring ambigrams are much easier to produce than standard ambigrams.

Ambigram application for shop-keepers: double the impact of your sale signs by using a *sale* ambigram ring. Only a total of eight *S*s are visible, but the word *sale* is hiding sixteen times in this ring. Of course, this ring works even better if what you are selling is *ale*.

Once you've got a chain ambigram, there are all sorts of games that you can play. Have a close look at the examples on this and the following page.

GO AND GO AND GO AND GO AND GO AND GO AND GO AND GO AND GO AND GO AND GO AND GO AND GO AND GO AND GO AND

Combining several copies of the same ring can give great results. For example, here the nested *singularity* rings combine into a picture that looks like a large singularity such as a black hole. Note also that two consecutive rings share their *i* dots, which means that there are no superfluous *i* dots in this ambigram vortex. Also, apart from being able to read the word *singularity* both in the clockwise and counter-clockwise directions along every ring, you can also read it going from the outside to the inside of the picture and from the inside to the outside by reading three letters on every ring before skipping to the next ring: sin-gul-ari-tys-ing-ula-rit- …

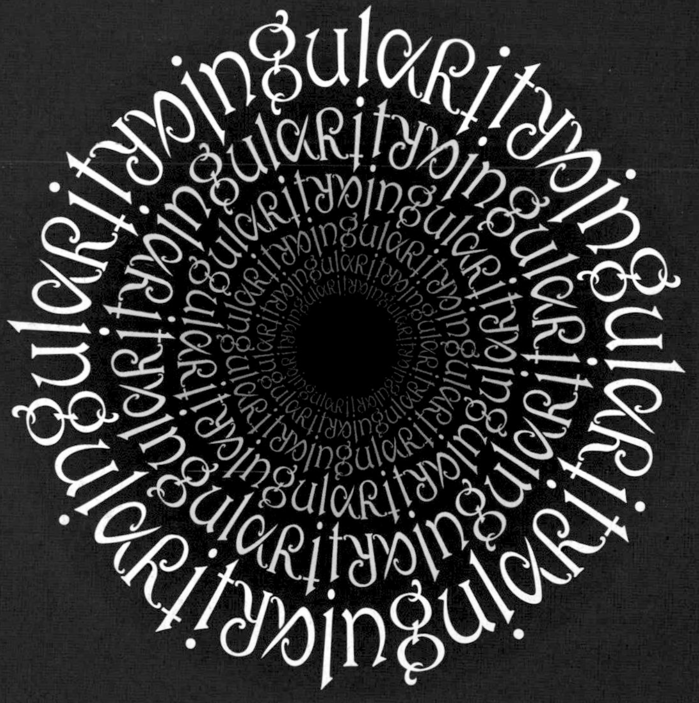

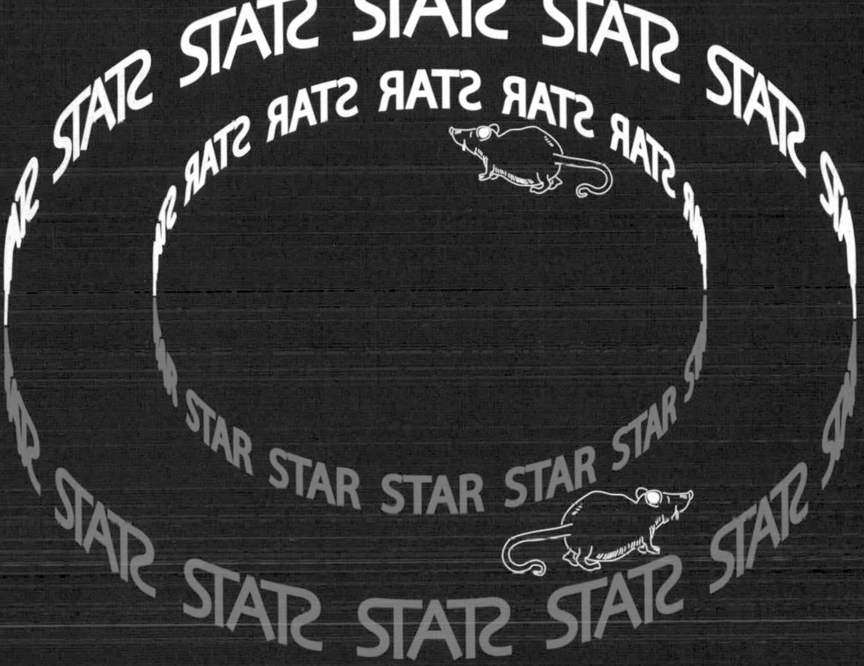

A different type of ring highlighting the mirror symmetry of the *star* ambigram. Somehow the rats snuck into my picture. Luckily John Langdon pointed them out to me.

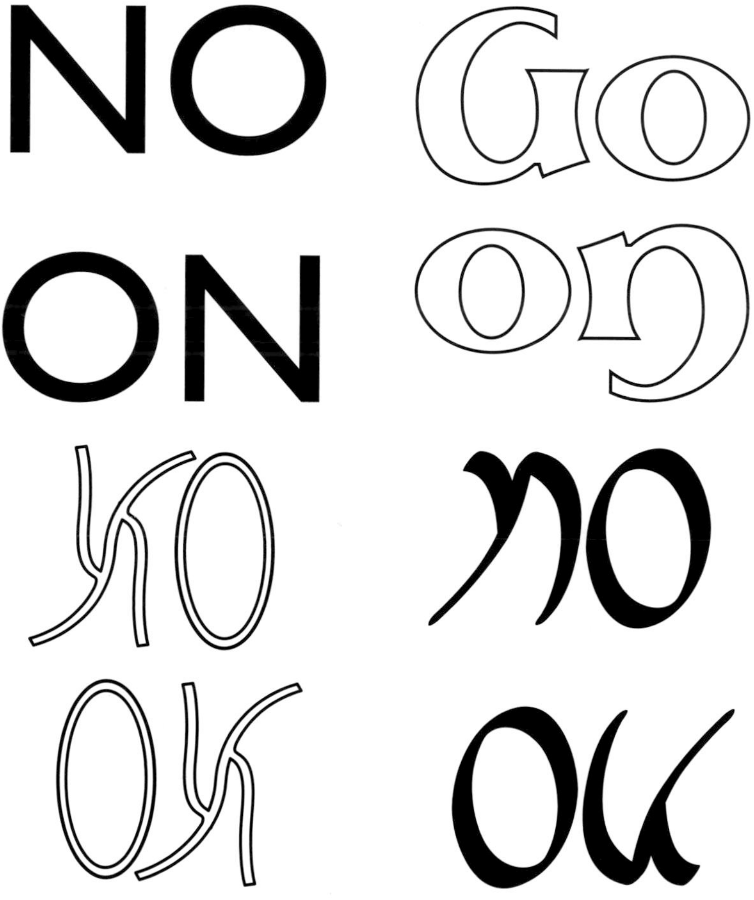

Geometrical ambigram variations around the letter *O*. Note that *Oz* is a common abbreviation for Australia and it is curious that a simple stick figure of a person turned on its side spells *ok*.

off

OH

HO

ON

OK

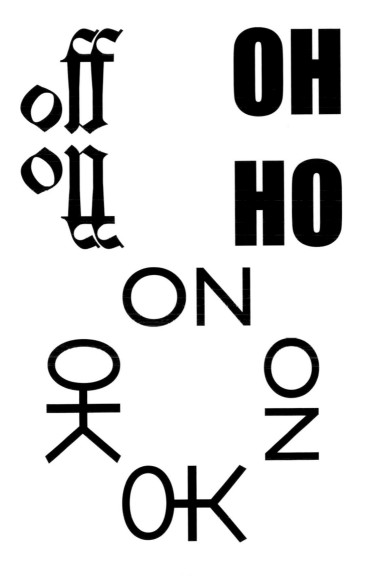

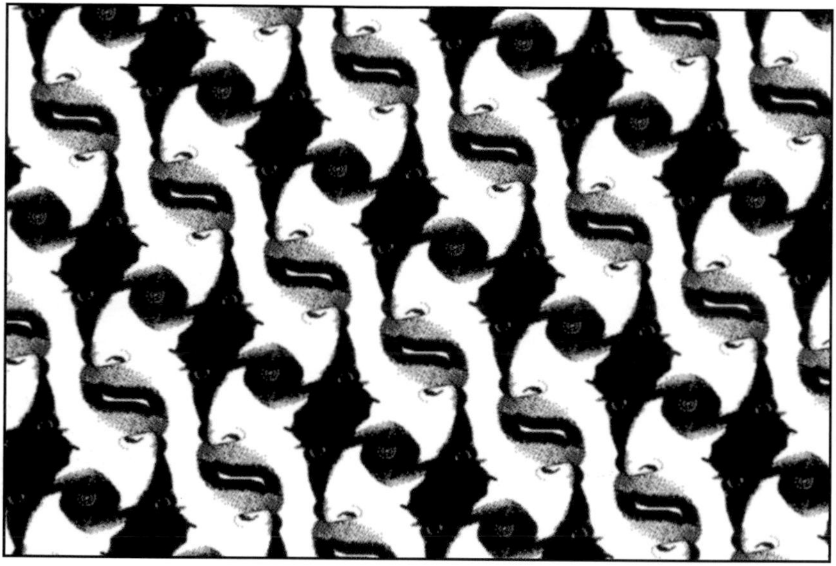

Geometrical ambigrams, especially those with identical readings, are very closely related to the kind of tessellations with animals that the famous Dutch artist M. C. Escher made popular. The *clown/horse tessellation* on the right is by Ken Landry. Tessellations like this are supposed to go on for ever on all sides. Just like a half-turn ambigram, this particular tessellation stays unchanged when you turn it upside-down. But, of course, there are a lot more 'coincidences' built into a drawing like this. The tessellation above is also by Ken Landry. It is made up of an infinite number of copies of Escher's face. All these faces are the right side up. What do you expect to see when you turn this page upside-down? Lots of upside-down faces? Well, go ahead, try it for yourself and be amazed.

INSIDE OUT

You are probably familiar with variations of the famous illusion shown above – depending on your frame of mind you either see a white vase or two black faces in profile facing each other

Figure/ground ambigrams work in the same way. John Langdon's ambigram *Us* below, is my favourite example. Can you see both the words *me* and *you*?

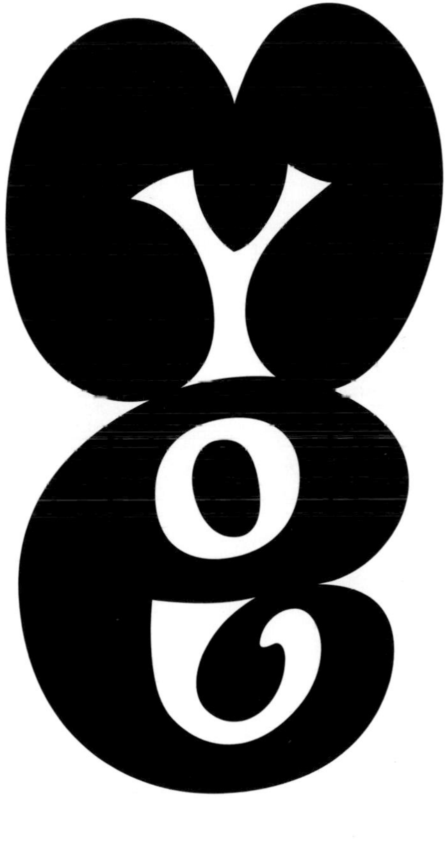

Other Types of Ambigrams and Related Visual Mayhem

In the main part of this book you will find many examples of the types of ambigrams described above and examples of other types of ambigrams. There is no complete list of all possible types of ambigrams as you can never be sure how many more interesting types are waiting to be discovered. However, if we are interested only in a rough classification, then the approach that Scott Kim takes in his book *Inversions* is probably the best. He gives a very concise classification of the principles on which various interesting types of ambigrams can be based. He distinguishes between ambigrams based on geometrical symmetries, perceptual mechanisms, and other organizing principles. For example, the half-turn and wall-reflection ambigrams described above are geometrical ambigrams, and the figure/ground ambigrams are perceptual ambigrams.

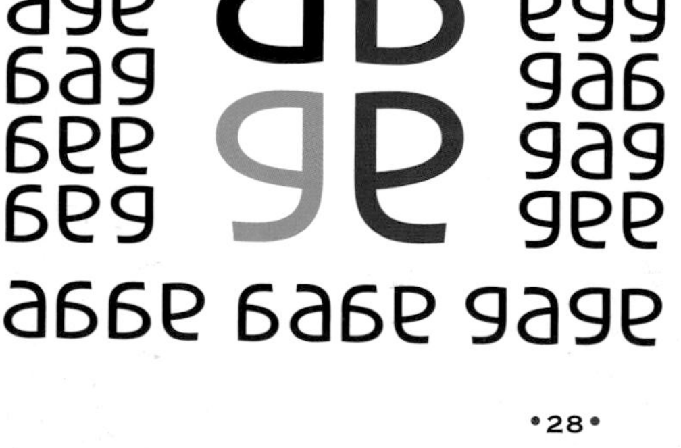

Ambiletters:
Depending on how you orient the letter a it reads as one of the letters a, b, e, or g. As you can see, there are quite a few words that are made up of these four letters.

BUOYANT FEAST

Wordplay: Did it ever occur to you that there is a *boat* hiding in *buoyant* or *fat* in *feast*? In this book you will also find lots of visually enhanced curiosities and games involving words that are not strictly ambigrams.

The very well-known ambiguous drawing by the British cartoonist W. H. Hill whose half-turn ambigram signature we encountered earlier. Can you see both the young and the old woman in the picture? There are also ambigrams that work like this picture – depending on your frame of mind you see one of two words; see some examples on pages 30, 31.

Here are a few more pieces by Douglas Hofstadter in which he explores a number of completely different ideas to turn words into ambigrams.

LIGHT IS A

Light is a *particle* or a *wave*, which depends on how you look at it, both in reality/physics and in the ambigram, left. The exclamation mark made up of a wave and a particle is also a nice touch.

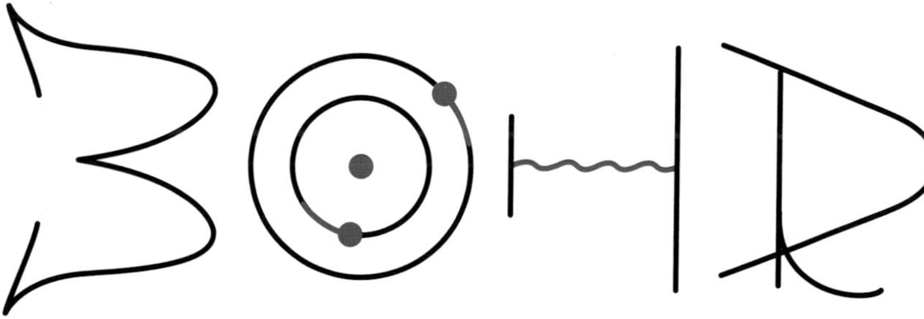

Turn *BOHR* one quarter-turn counter-clockwise to get his *ATOM*. The *O* in *BOHR* represents the Bohr atom (hydrogen) itself, showing a proton with two different electron orbits around it, while the *H* represents the transition between the two orbits in the standard way that energy levels and transitions between them are depicted in physics.

Doug created his rainbow ambigram on the left in 2006. The signature reads simultaneously *Doug* and *2006*. All the words in the rainbow are not quite mirror images of themselves. Still the rainbow reads the same in a mirror. Can you spot the differences between the rainbow and its mirror image?

Escher & Co.

If you really like M. C. Escher's magical drawings but are a little bit tired of seeing the same pictures over and over again reproduced on mugs, calendars and the like, you're in for a treat in this section. On the following pages, you will see some brand-new twists to some of Escher's most famous drawings.

The tessellation on the left is by Ken Landry.

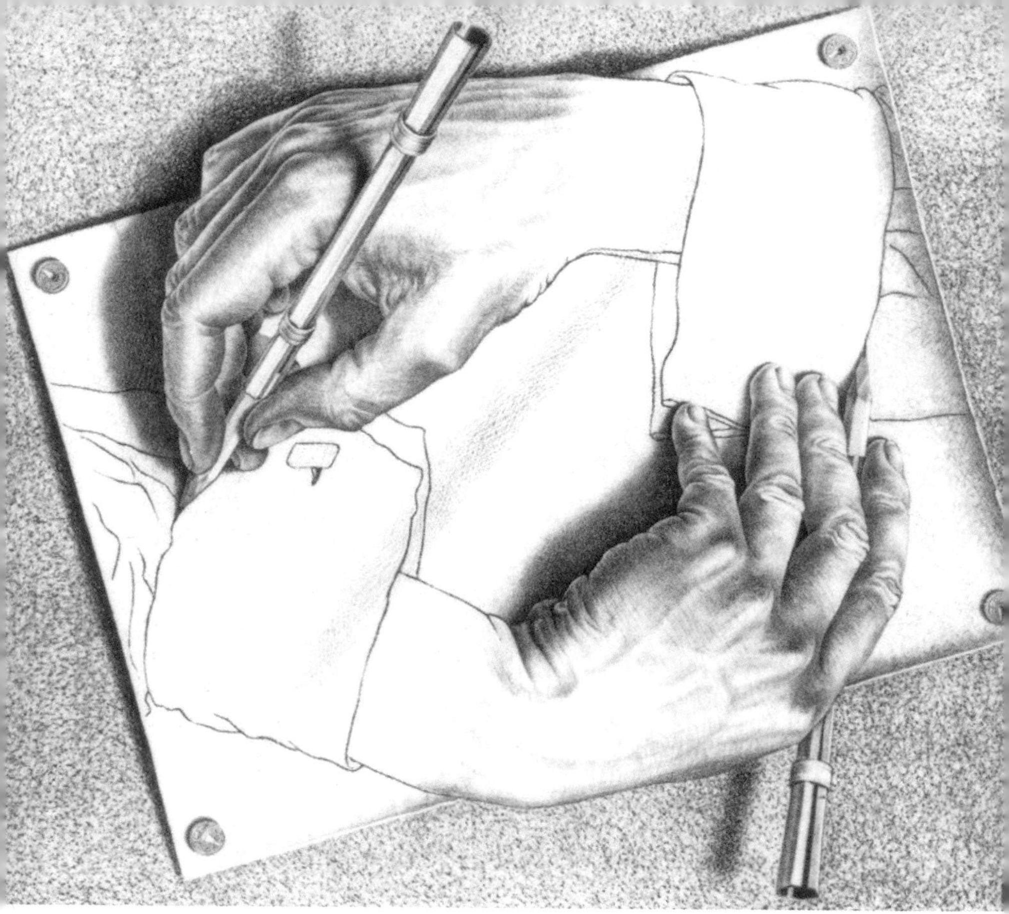

Escher's *Drawing Hands* shows two hands that draw each other. The hands are slightly different. However, if you look at this drawing upside-down you still get the same overall impression. The picture on the right has been modified in such a way that the hands simultaneously write the half-turn ambigram of the name *Escher*.

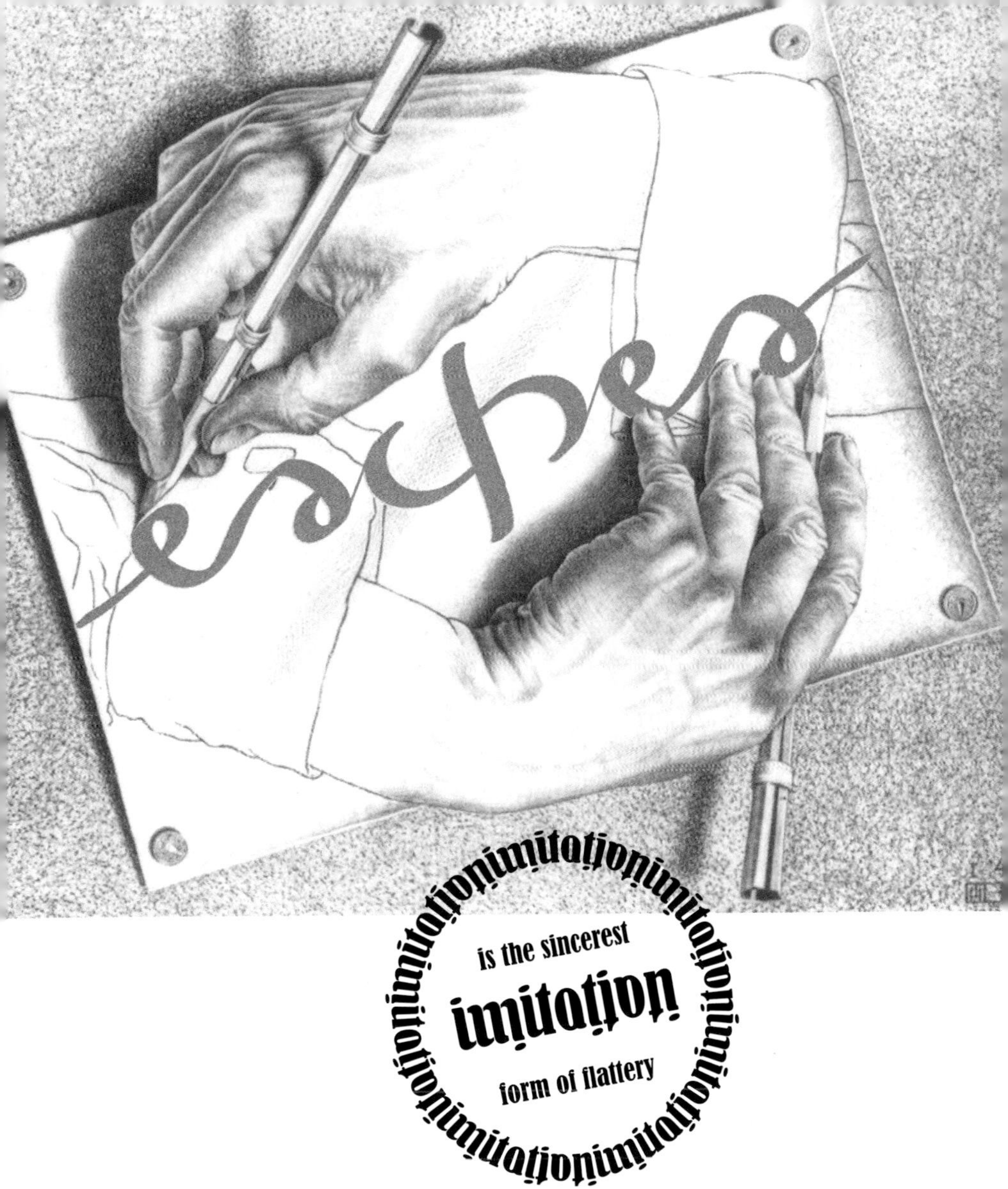
escher
imitationimitationimitationimitation
is the sincerest
imitation
form of flattery

Escher's drawing *Magic Mirror* (see above) is based on mirror symmetry. The ambigram of *mirror* that I have superimposed on the right is due to Scott Kim. I only added the *magic* to ambigrammatically capture the name of the drawing. The drawing also features winged lions that seem to materialize at the end of the mirror close to us. As one lion prowls along the mirror, it splits up into two winged lions, one the mirror image of the other. Both lions then proceed to promenade around the spheres. Gradually they turn from being solid three-dimensional creatures into flat two-dimensional ones, which combine into a fantastic tessellation.

mirror

In Escher's drawing *Day and Night* (above) the landscape on the left is the (negative) mirror image of the landscape on the right. One side shows the scene at night, the other one the same scene during the day. Of course, there is also the amazing tessellation with black and white birds morphing into the tessellation with black and white square fields.

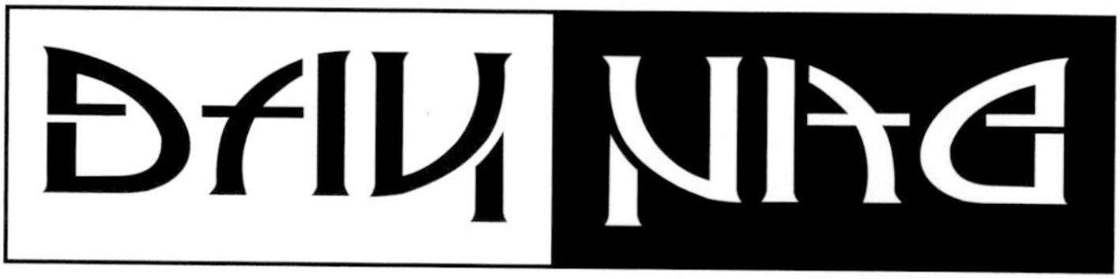

In this ambigrammatic counterpart of Escher's drawing the left side *day* is the mirror image of the right side *nite*.

Are you one of the few people who have noticed that there is a difference in shape between the black and white birds? The white birds who are flying into the night are tired, indicated by their tails pointing down. The tails of the black birds, who have just woken up and and have the day ahead of them, are pointing up.

Hop David's painting *Rams* was inspired by Escher's drawing. Unlike Escher's drawing, it is built around a half-turn symmetry and the tessellation in its centre is one with black and white rams.

Alain Nicolas's tessellation with a caricature silhouette of Escher.

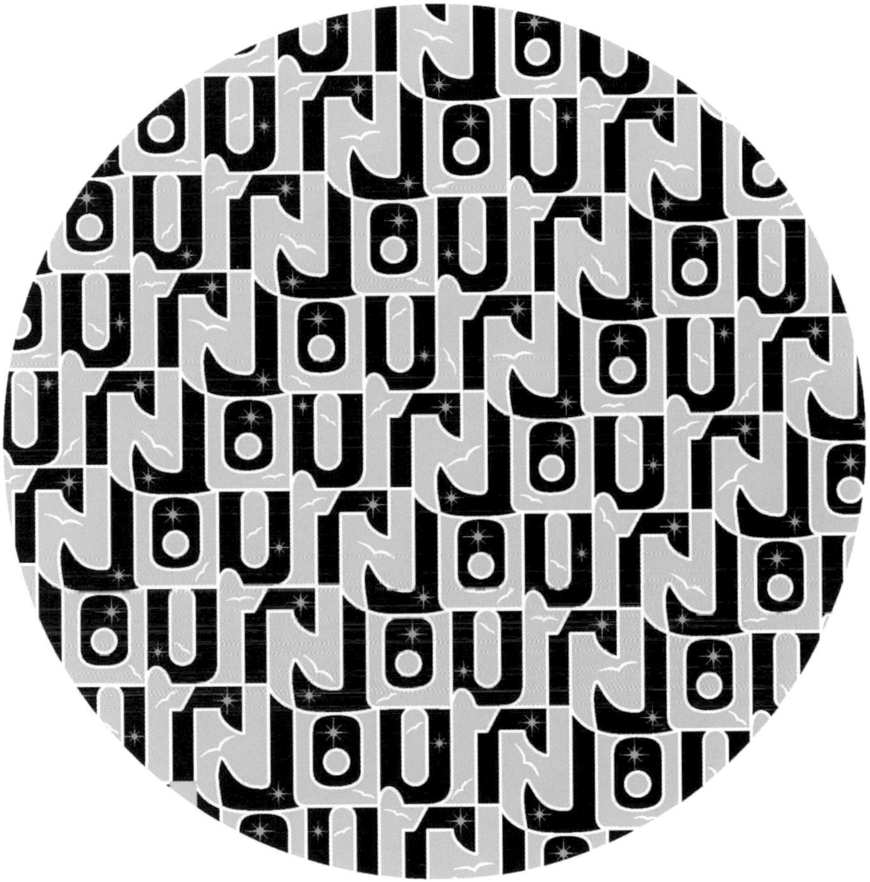

Paradoxe Jour/Nuit

Another tessellation by Alain Nicolas with the two French words for day (*jour*) and night (*nuit*).

VII-'53

Without the figures in Escher's drawing *Relativity*, the building would look a little strange. However, there is really nothing impossible about it. Things take a decidedly weird turn once you realize, after looking at the different figures, that gravity is pulling in three different directions and that there are three different 'up's in this scene. John Langdon's elegant *Relativity* and *Gravity* ambigrams capture the title and what is going on in this drawing. Of course, the ambigrams 'only' have two ups each.

Hop David's amazing painting *Dragons* is based on a tessellation featuring a transformation of two-dimensional dragons into three-dimensional dragons, and back again.

This *dragon* ambigram ring tries to capture some of the magical circular transformation in the painting. Also note the 2 with the blocked-out middle at the top of the ring magically turning into a 3 with its middle blocked out at the bottom of the ring. This is supposed to mimic the transition from 2- to 3-dimensional dragons and back.

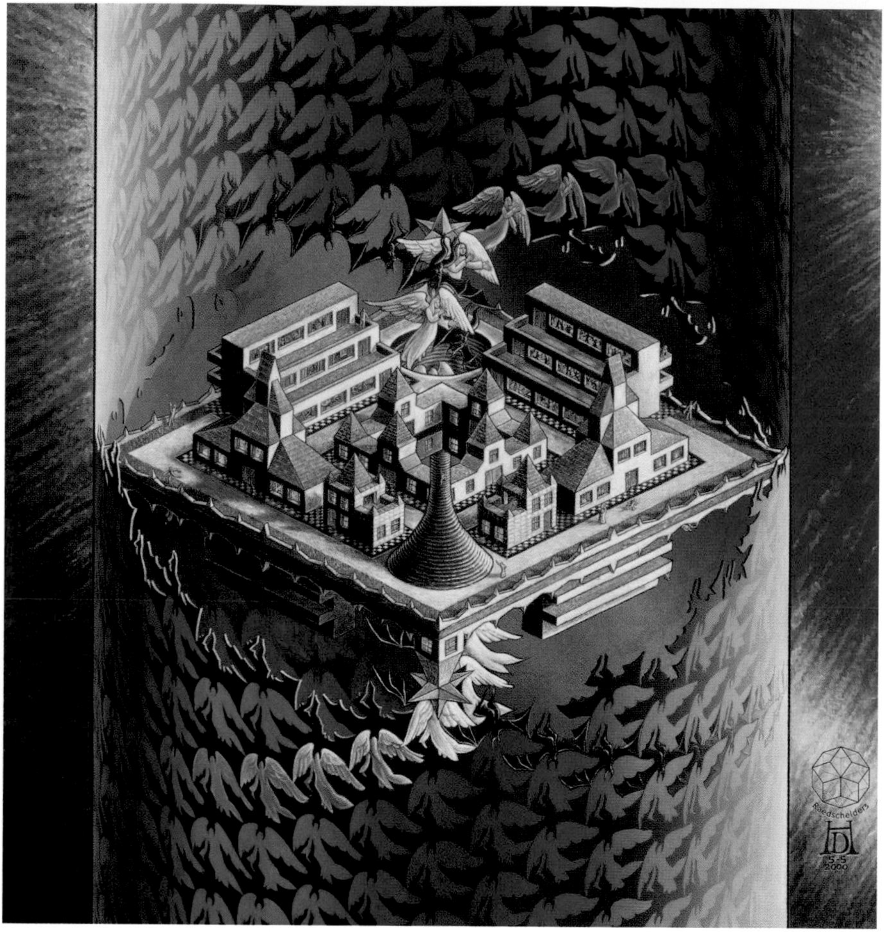

In the painting *The Tunnel* Hop David fuses his tessellation *Angels and Devils* and Peter Raedschelders's drawing *Impossible City*. In the ambigram I've tried to imitate this fusion. The first line reads *Impossible* and the second line, which is the first line upside-down, reads *angels&devils*.

Impossible

On the left is Hop David's *Angels and Devils* tessellation twisted into an eternal descent into hell or, if you are an optimist, an eternal ascent to heaven. Above, John Langdon's masterpiece *Angels & Demons*.

Alain Nicolas's tesselation *Plouf* has an infinite number of frogs jumping towards the middle of the picture.

In this vortex which is based on an ambigram ring by John Langdon the words do the acrobatics. It can be read in two different ways: ... *no end no end* ... and ... *on and on and on* .... Both readings are contained in each of the rings – just read in clockwise and counter-clockwise directions. Both readings also jump out if you read along the spokes of the wheel. Diving in from the top ... *no end* ... and from the bottom ... *on and on* ...

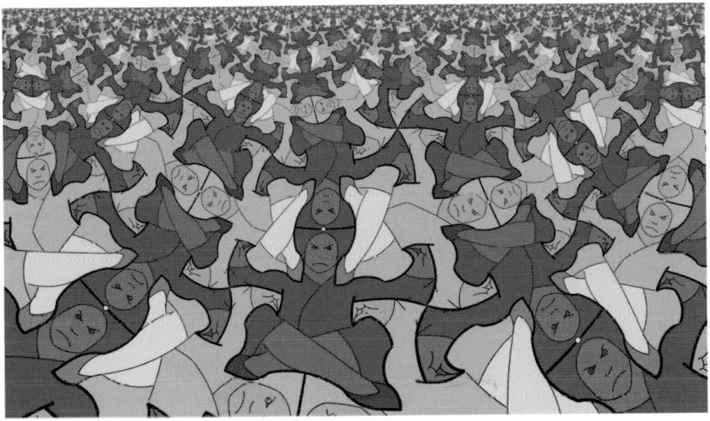

Two attempts at capturing infinity in a finite area by Jos Leys. I have tried to keep both from exploding by adding a *limiting* ring ambigram and *limiting* chain ambigrams. Added twist: the kind of acrobatics that the turtles are performing is usually called a *circle limit*.

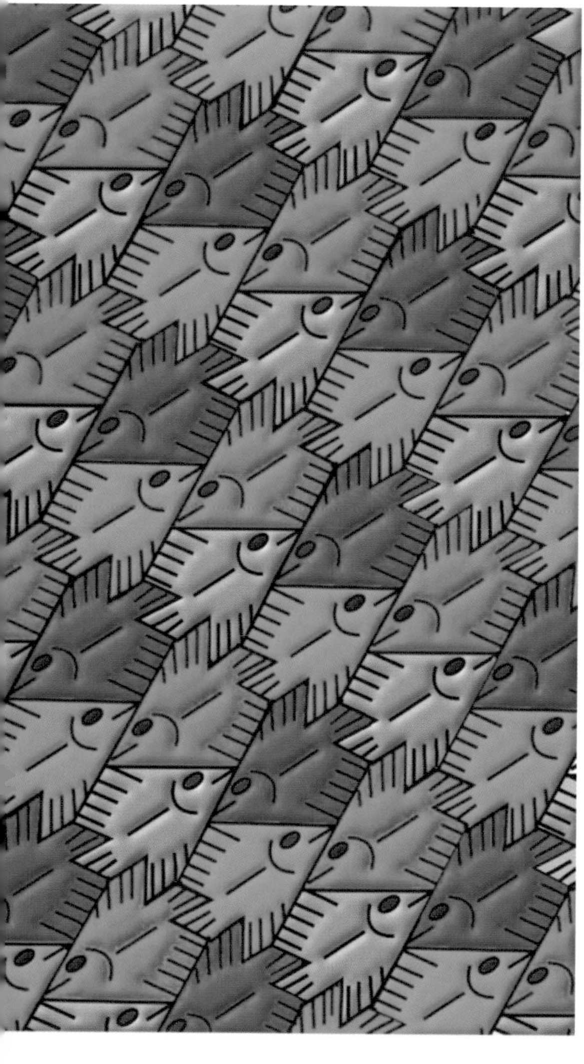

Now here is a very special two-way fish tile designed by William E. Wenger. Using only copies of this tile there are just two ways to fill a plane ocean. Escher times two! I recycled the ambigram of the word *way* from John Langdon's *Wordplay* ambigram (see page 1).

may

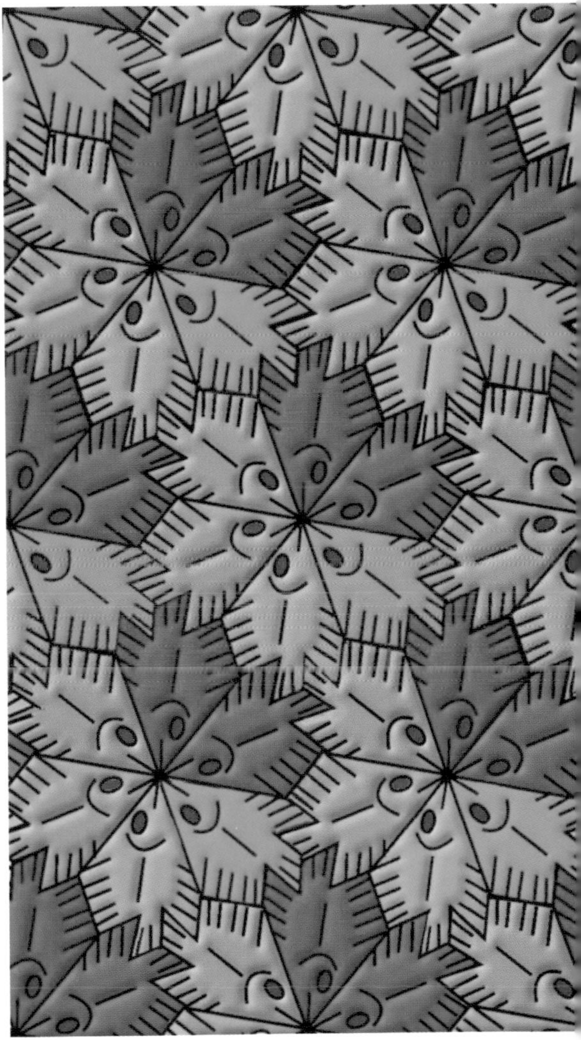

Topsy Turvy

One of the easiest ways to get a new angle on a familiar object is to turn it

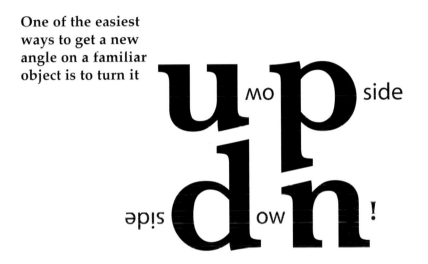

When you try this trick with half-turn ambigrams you end up with one of two extremes – either the ambigram stays unchanged, or it really looks and reads completely differently, very much like this upside-down cartoon by Gustave Verbeek (it shows an owl the right side up and two men sleeping under a haystack upside-down).

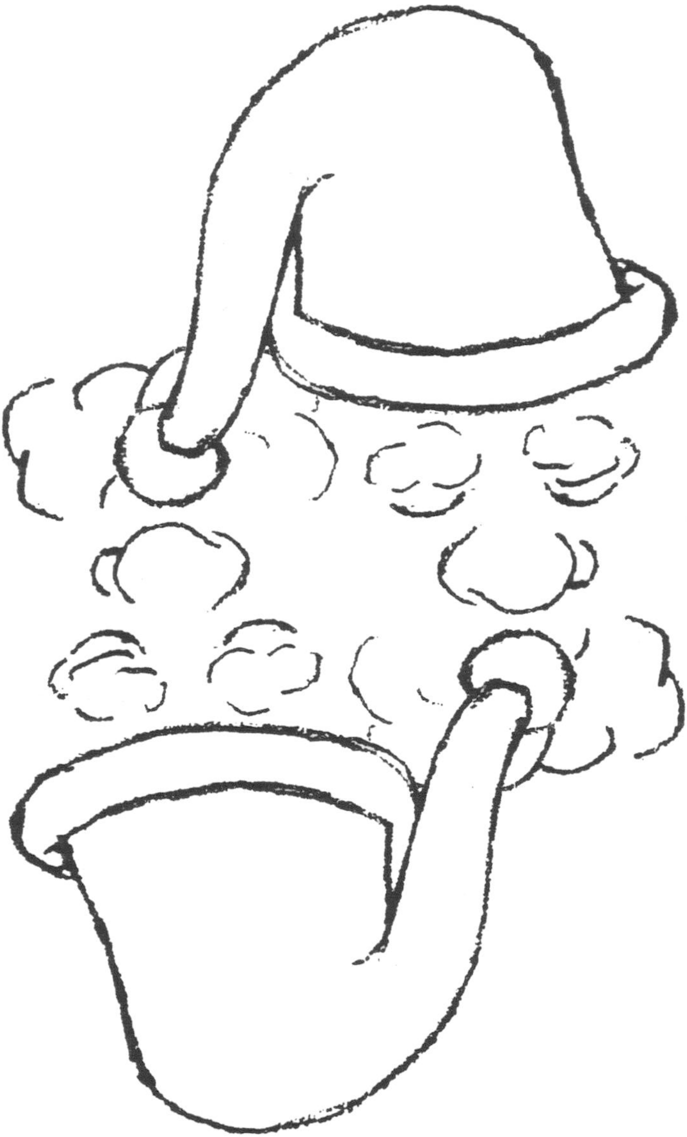

As for this marvellous *Christmas* ambigram by Brett Gilbert, the vast majority of ambigrams are half-turn ambigrams featuring exactly the same reading both the right side up and upside-down. On the other hand, virtually all upside-down heads exhibit two or more very different characteristics. Paul Agule's *Santa Claus*, who almost seems to be a pipe dream of himself, is a very rare exception.

Can you see one person whispering into another person's ear? Twice? Both the right side up and upside-down – one in black and the other in white? This drawing is a variation of an illustration that appeared on the title pages of a number of bilingual specialist dictionaries published by Peter Collin Publishing. *Hearsay* is the perfect title for this picture, written as a half-turn ambigram, of course.

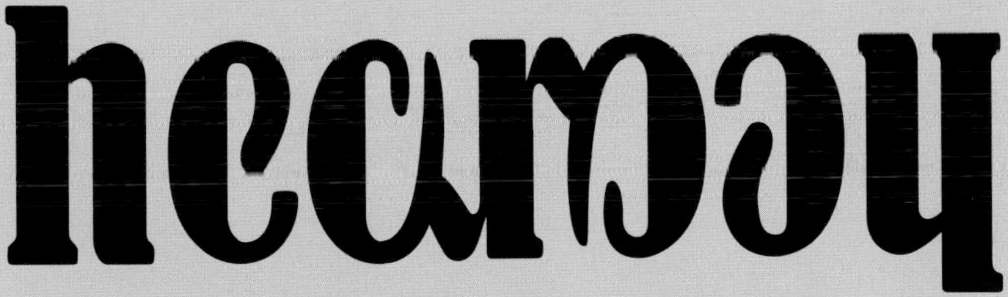

1981

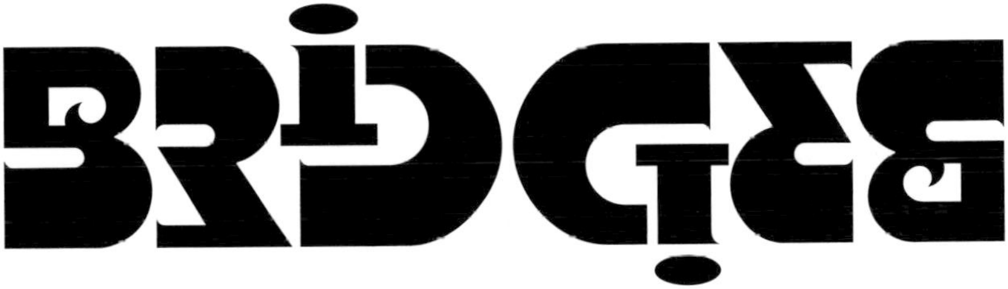

John Langdon fuses two identical bridges into one upside-down *bridges* ambigram, and Sandro Del-Prete succeeds in doing something very similar with two different diametrically opposed views of an actual bridge in his drawing *The Railway Bridge*.

Alice's adventures in

WONDERLAND

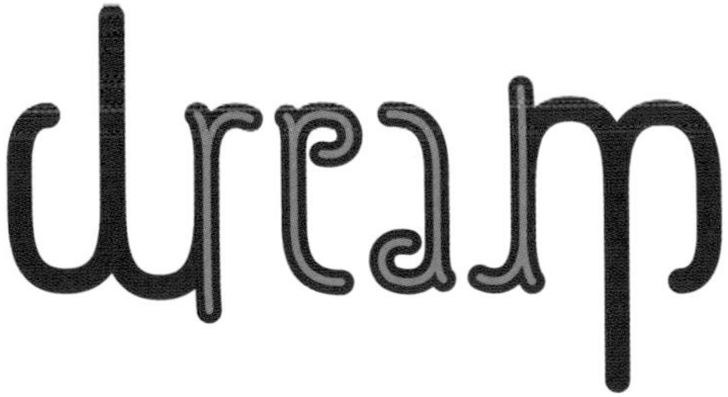

Just a dream or real?

The *wonderland* ambigram is by Kevin Pease, and the illustrations are by John Tenniel.

BEWARE!

A man in a canoe, a deserted island and a fish frolicking in the ocean. However, danger lurks just one half-turn away. The illustration is taken from one of Gustave Verbeek's amazing upside-down cartoons. John Langdon's ambigram spells out the right kind of advice – both ways. On closer inspection, even the first scene is not so idyllic. The man in the canoe looks scared by the huge fish, whose rear fin is about to hit the water.

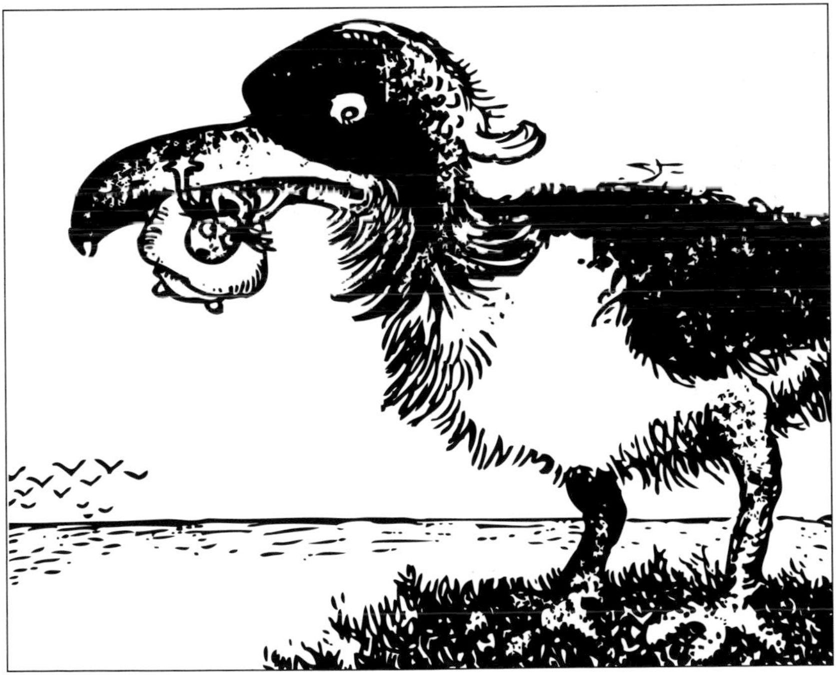

dn

up

There are at least three very different amazing things happening when you go from one panel to the other by turning it upside-down.

- First, of course, you can admire an amazing vintage Japanese upside-down head in action – a happy old man turning into a very unhappy old man after performing a simple headstand.

- The happy face looks down, whereas the unhappy face looks up. The natural ambigram pair *up/d(ow)n* is supposed to comment on this. However, there is more.

- When you look closely, you will notice that the *up* seems to be jutting out of the page whereas the *d(ow)n* seems to be carved into the page. This is an optical illusion based on the way we are used to interpreting shadows.

Alain Nicolas takes the idea of an upside-down head one step further by filling the whole plane with copies of such a head. *Gentil/Méchant* is the French title of this amazing tessellation. Robert Maitland's ambigram *volte face* comments on the diametrically opposed characters of this 'dual persona'.

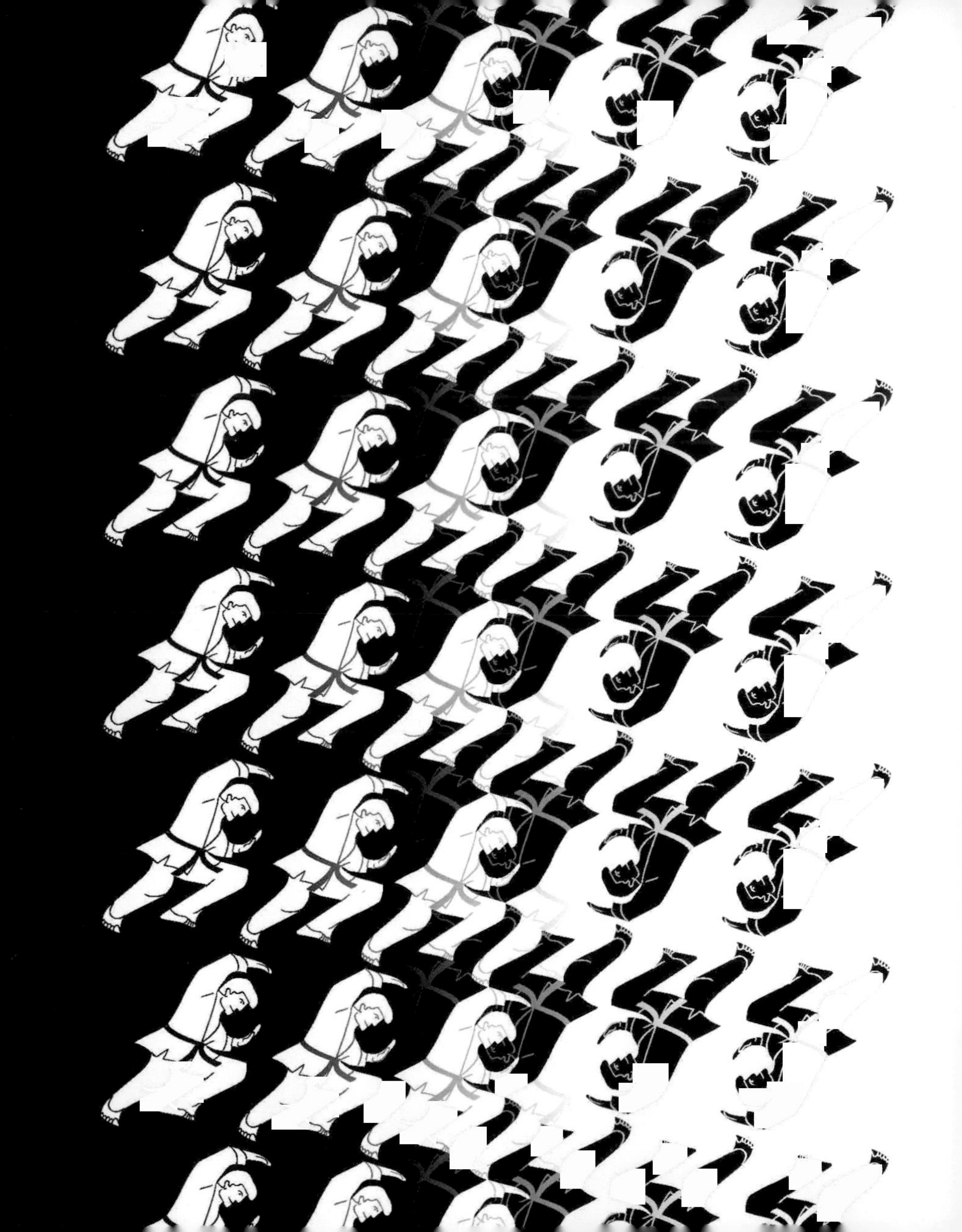

How 'close' can 'close combat' get? Have a look at Alain Nicolas's 'judo' tessellation and you will see.

And, how tightly should you 'Seize the Day'? Follow John Langdon's example and you cannot go wrong.

Imagine a Night is the title of a marvellous children's book illustrated by Rob Gonsalves. The painting on the right, entitled *Ladies of the Lake*, is the illustration on the jacket of this book. The wonderful ambigram is by Kevin Pease.

Infinitely Many Questions by Renato and Roberto Fernandez. Do you see an infinity sign or two question marks?

The answer to all these questions: 42 in two ways. Or is it ten different ways? You can read forty-two four times around the ring in the clockwise direction, another four times in the counter-clockwise direction and, of course, you can also read 42 twice. These two ambigrams are by Brett Gilbert.

mind
mindmatter
matter

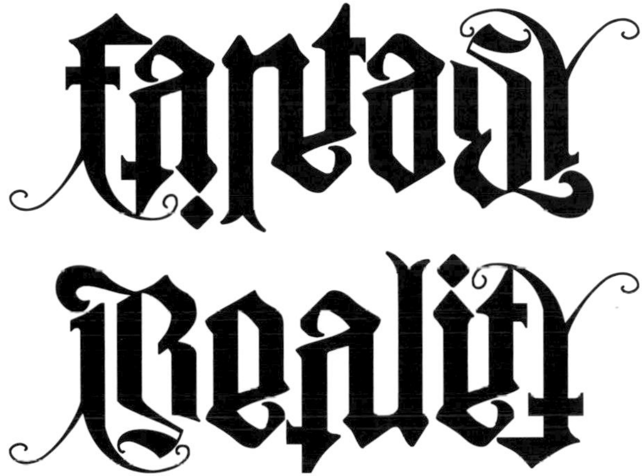

My *Mind Over Matter* and *Mindmatter* and two versions of *Fantasy/Reality*; the one above by Mark Palmer and the one below by Robert Maitland.

John Langdon's classic *No Limitations* spiral above, commenting on my little daughter Lara performing a very special twisting trick. To make the illusion, I cut the Lara ring on the left as shown and distorted it to fit repeatedly and seamlessly into a logarithmic spiral.

So, you think of yourself as an ambigrammist? The only problem is that your name is *Burkard Polster*. Working ambigrams usually rely heavily on the words they represent being very familiar. So is it at all possible to make an ambigram of a name, neither of whose two parts will be familiar to anybody in the English-speaking world? I let you be the judge. Above is my own attempt and on the right three versions of John Langdon's amazing calligraphic firework.

Mirror Mirror on the Wall

Art is Life by Robert Petrick

When you look in the mirror you never see yourself as others see you unless you have a perfectly symmetrical face. Studies have shown that to some extent

symmetry = beauty

The more symmetrical a face the more beautiful it is perceived to be. Does this also apply to ambigrams? To find out have a look at the perfectly symmetrical ambigrams in this chapter.

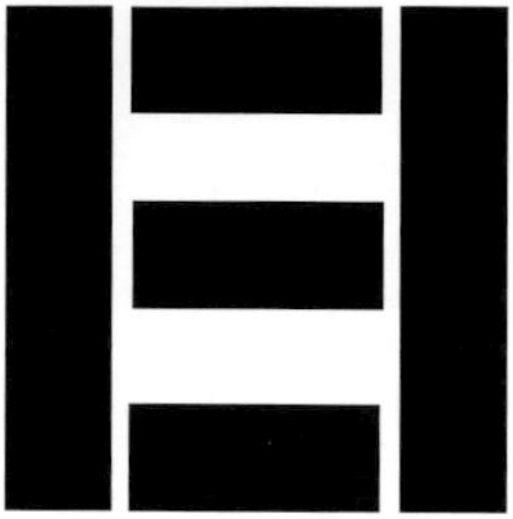

The ambigrams on this page stay unchanged no matter how you reflect or turn them. *Ei* is the German word for egg, one of the most perfect shapes (too bad the ambigram is square). Then there is *CD* at the bottom. Finally, the ideal *Ideal* is by Robert Petrick.

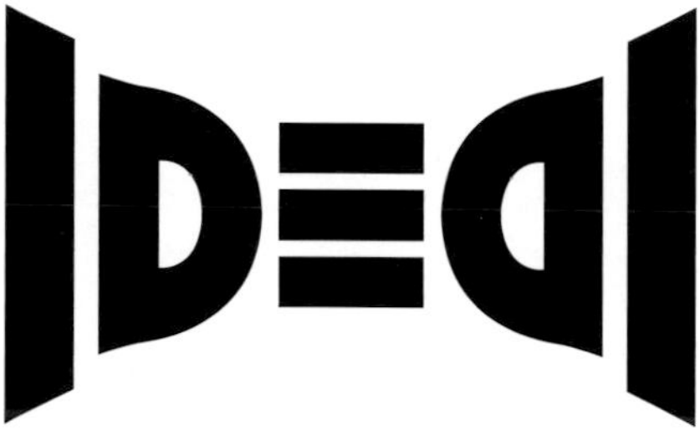

In John Langdon's network at every junction you are given a *CHOICE* and you can *DECIDE* to go up, or you can *DECIDE* to go down.

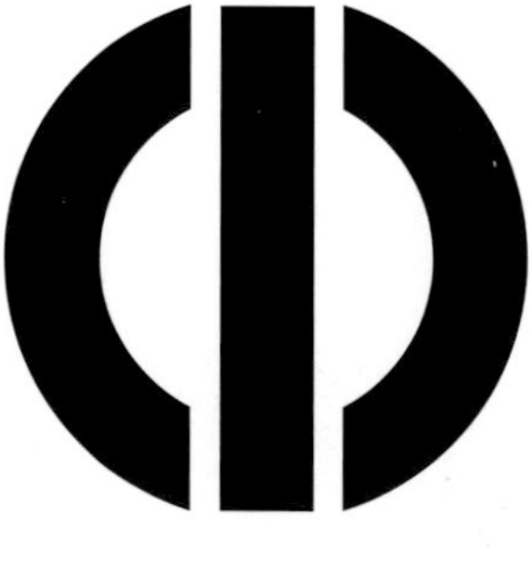

CHOICE
DECIDE

My Metaphysical Mirror (front) by John Langdon, discovered while playing fun word games with familiar corporate logos.

My Metaphysical Mirror (back)

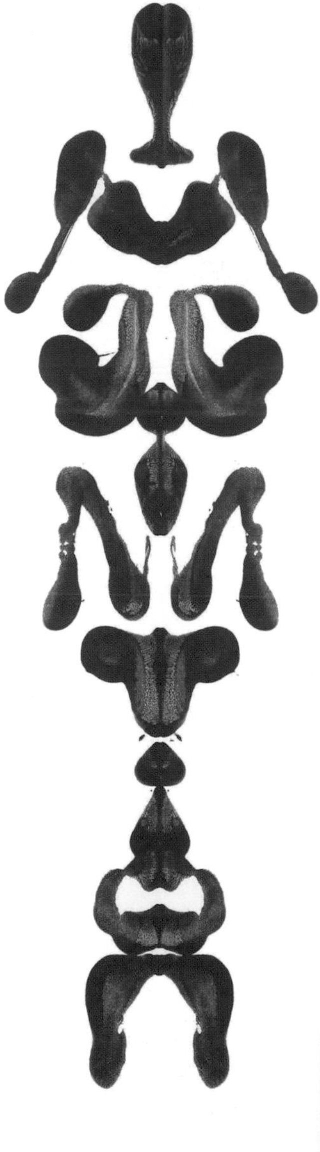

Inkblot test: what do you see in the top inkblot? A devil's face? A headless person? What do you make of the bottom inkblot ambigram by Kevin Pease? And what is John Langdon trying to tell you on the right? Hint: use your imagination to decipher this one. (See page 221 for the solutions.)

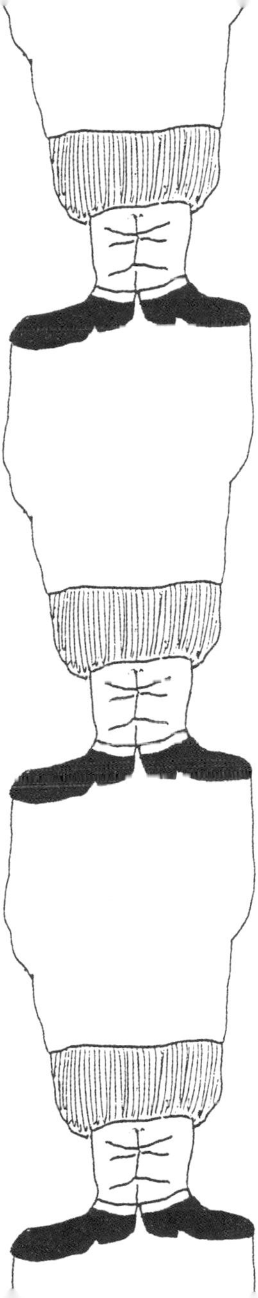

The Man Who Stands on His Own Shoulders by Paul Agule.

As you can see, one can make up a similar symmetrical chain using the word *DECODE*. What is decoded here? Of course, the many *CODE*s that make up this chain!

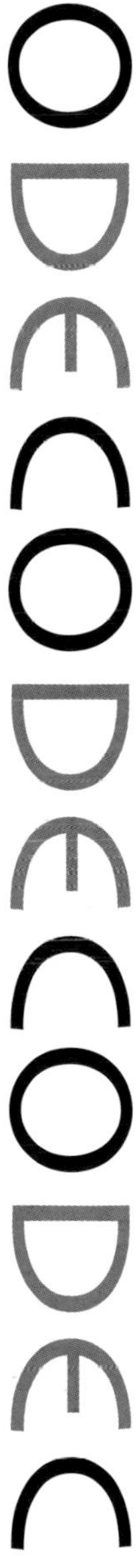

Robert Petrick has evolved the word *Evolve* into the ambigram above which is its own mirror image. Did it ever occur to you that the first four letters of *evolve* are the word *love* backwards? In this ambigram you can read this word both forwards and backwards. A nice second layer of ambiguity which I have tried to isolate in the ring on the right and the two chains below.

lovelovelovelove

evolvevolvevolv

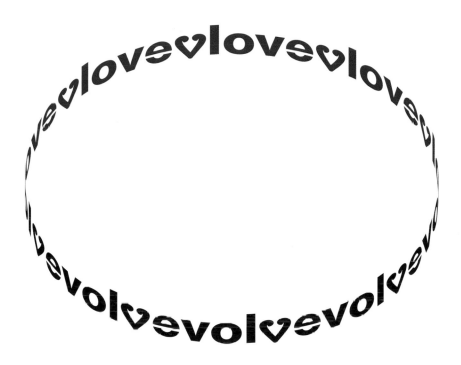

evolvevolvevolv

Inside Out

What is next once you are sick of mirrors and have turned everything in sight upside-down? Turn everything inside-out, of course.

To whet your appetite start with a *Folkmanis* caterpillar hand puppet which turns into a butterfly when you invert it, but then proceed straight to the ambigrams.

Us by John Langdon.
us = me + you

A simple *me* that turns into a *we* in two different ways

In *St George and the Dragon* by Sandro Del-Prete, the valiant St George is fighting it out with the dragon. At the same time you can get a close-up of St George's face by focusing on the negative space of the fighting scene. Punya Mishra's ambigram *Good and Evil* provides an alternative title and packs the two words *good* and *evil* in a similar fashion.

Slave Market with Disappearing Bust of Voltaire by Salvador Dalí. Your mission is to find both the slave market and Voltaire (see page 221 for the solution).

The Persistence of Influence by John Langdon. Your mission is to find both the words 'Salvador' and 'Dalí'.

LA VIE EN ROSE
"La vie en rose"
Sandro Del-Prete 1994

Left: Sandro Del-Prete's *Flourishing of the Rose*. Can you see both the rose and the lovers hiding in the rose?

ROSEROSEROSERO

Depending on where you start reading the infinite string ... *OSEROSEROSE* ... above you see *ROSE* or *EROS*. The ambigram below has two similar related readings: *Love* and *Dove*.

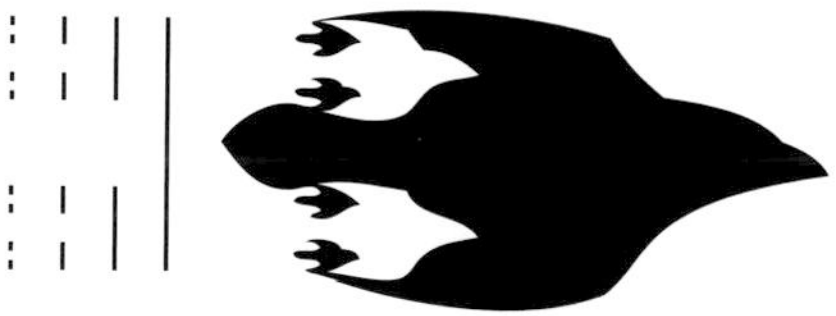

7 Birds, a painting by Hop David. How many birds do you see? Only five? Where are the two missing birds hiding? See page 221 for the solution if you cannot find them. This painting also attempts to suggest infinity. A line drawn from wing tip to wing tip of one of the birds has its middle third cut out by the tail feathers. If you were to add more and more birds as suggested, you could get an infinite set of points known as the *Cantor Set*.

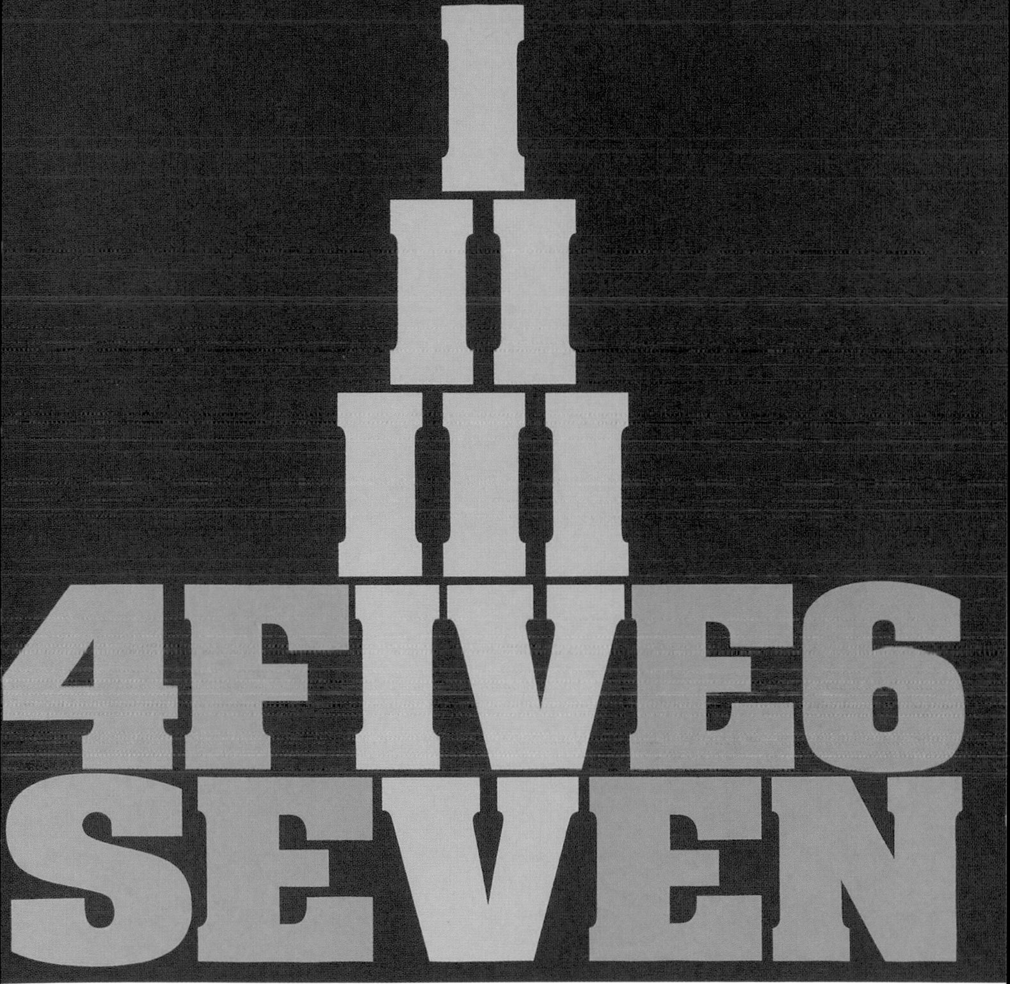

Years and Years, a painting by John Langdon. How many numbers can you spot? As you can see, context is very important when it comes to interpreting what we see. In a good ambigram those letters that are easily recognizable will provide enough context to make the rest of the ambigram stick together.

Canada: the French and the English – love or hate? The answer is hidden in the Canadian flag. The negative image of the leaf contains profiles of two angry men, Jack and Jacques, yelling at each other (see page 221 if you cannot spot the faces).

One of the most amazing optical illusions ever created. By John Langdon, of course.

The amazing figure/ground *love/hate* ambigram is by John Langdon.

The drawing *Inner Beauty* by J. D. Hillberry shows the illusion of notebook paper taped to some wood. The subject of the rose speaks to the illusion of beauty. True beauty is always below the surface and true love is the ability to see the beauty within. The entire image was drawn, including the tape, paper and wooden background.

What word do you see when you look at the text above? Flat? Look again. This is a Magic Eye stereogram. Once you succeed in merging the two lines at the top with your eyes, you will see the word *3D* popping out right in the middle of the picture. This image was created with Julius Kammerl's ASCII stereogram generator.

Foreign Fonts

Here is a great idea. Why not write an ambigram story that is its own translation into another language – 'just' write each word as a half-turn ambigram that reads like the word in English and like the word in the other language when you turn it upside-down. Even though this is basically impossible, ambigram artists have played with this idea ...

To translate the two handwritten Chinese words for *China* and *Tokyo* into English turn the page ninety degrees in the clockwise direction. The ambigrams on this and the following two pages are by David Moser.

To translate these two Chinese words for *sea* and *America* a quarter-turn in the anti-clockwise direction is all that is needed.

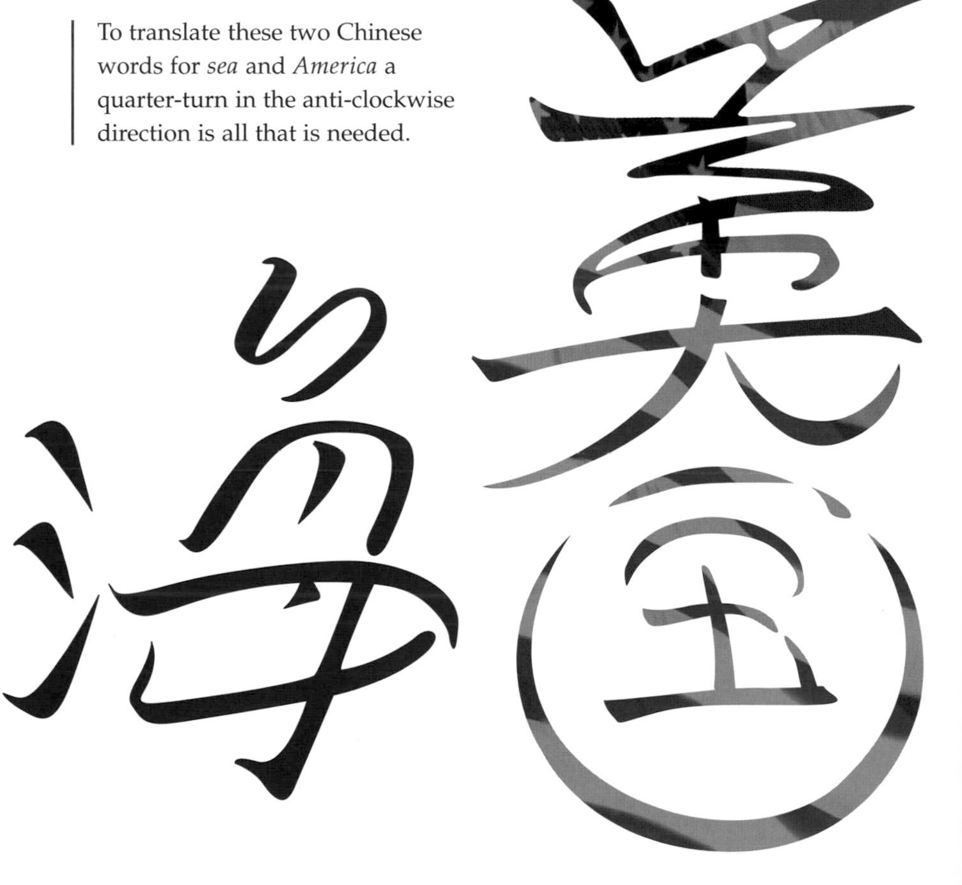

Looking at this ambigram a Chinese person will most likely see only a handwritten version of the two Chinese characters 中國 spelling out the word *China*. On the other hand, anybody who is more familiar with our alphabet will immediately see the English word *China*.

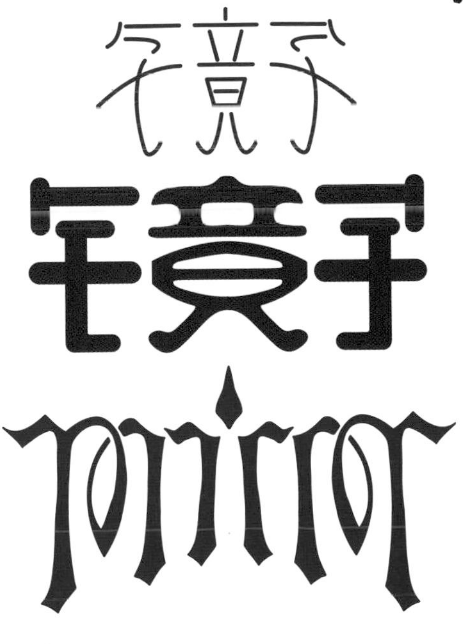

Three mirrors that are their own mirror image! Two wall-reflection ambigrams of the Chinese word for mirror and Scott Kim's marvellous English *mirror* ambigram underneath.

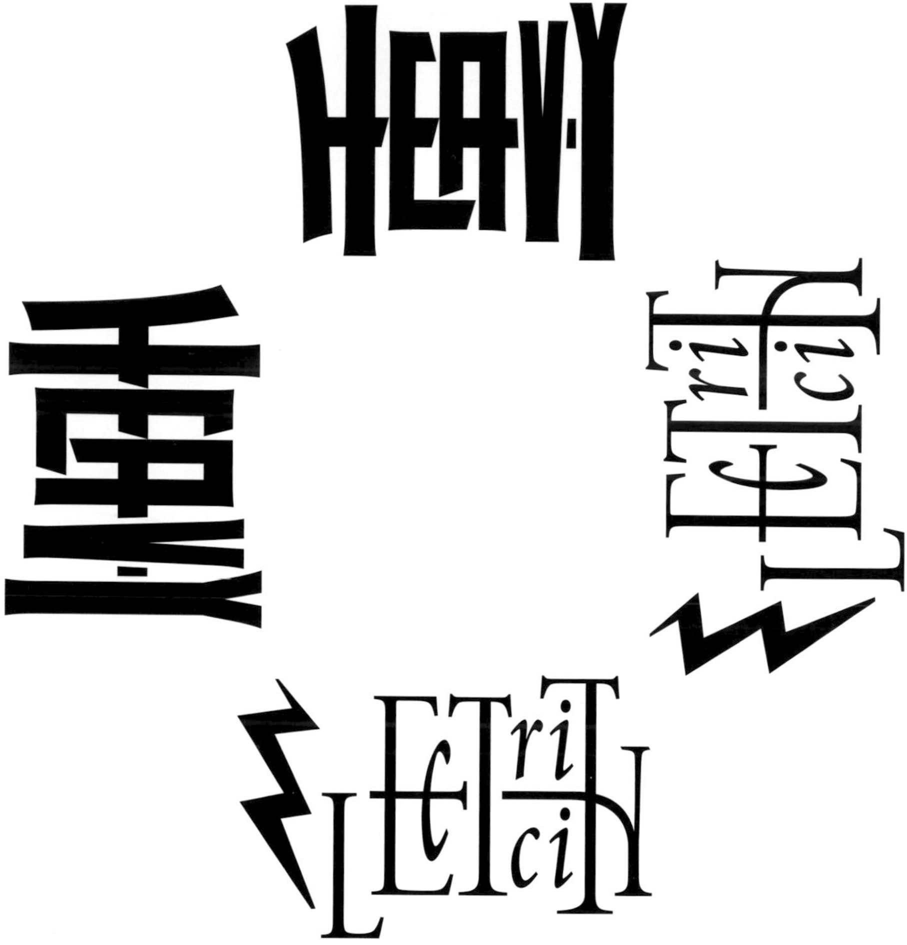

Three ambigrams by Scott Kim commissioned by the Japanese Tenyo Company who used the images on their mobile phone magic trick website. Above, *heavy* and *electricity* in kanji and in English. On the right, *ureshii* turning into *kanasii* (Japanese for *happy* and *sad*).

Ureshii

Kanashii

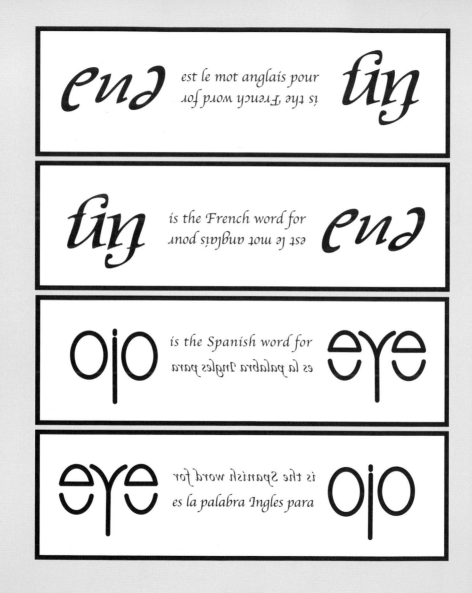

end est le mot anglais pour fin

is the French word for

fin is the French word for end

est le mot anglais pour

ojo is the Spanish word for eye

es la palabra Ingles para

is the Spanish word for

eye es la palabra Ingles para ojo

OUI
PVJ
QWK
RXL
SYM
TZN
UAO
VBP
WCQ
XDR
YES

Translation from *French to English*: one letter at a time. Other interesting pairs of words that are linked in this way include: cold-frog, jerk-fang, ugly-oats, pens-etch, hush-bomb, IBM-HAL (the evil computer in the movie *2001: A Space Odyssey*).

ETHETHETHETHETHET
ETHETHETHETHETHET

English to Dutch by letter shift

STATE-ÉTATS

English to French by letter reversal

MINE-MEIN-MIEN

English to German to French by letter shuffle

OUI-AYE OUI-YEA

These French and English pairs of words for 'Yes' both contain all six vowels and no consonants. Translation by vowel complement?

dead
alive

Life Beyond Ambigrams

Is there life and play in words beyond ambigrams? You bet!

Bin Laden – Dead or Alive
by Roberto Fernandez

Somebody who has got *Liar* written all over his face, by Paul Agule. Conceived in a flash while listening to someone lying to him on the phone.

A charade is a set of words formed by respacing but not rearranging the letters of another word, phrase or sentence. The two charades printed in blue are special in that they have opposite meanings to their counterparts printed in red. Most of the examples shown here can be found in *The Dictionary of Wordplay* by Dave Morice.

nowhere
nowhere
nowhere
nowhere
now here
now here

BEDEVIL

MENSWEAR

FRIEDRICH

BED
BEDEVIL
EVIL

an ISLAND ... IS LAND

a DAREDEVIL is one
who DARED EVIL

SEA RINGS UNLIT ISLAND
SEA RINGS UNLIT ISLAND
SEA RINGS UN LIT ISLAND
SEA RING SUN LIT ISLAND
SEARING SUN LIT ISLAND
SEARING SUN LIT ISLAND

Paul Agule in anti-war action on the left and John Langdon above.

Das Sechskantquadra(d)
Die Quadratur des Rades
a
b
A
B
C
D
Sandro Del-Prete 1969

Quadrature of the Wheel by Sandro Del-Prete, complemented by my *Squaring the Circle* ambigram. Ever since the ancient Greek geometers came up with the challenge, people have been trying to square the circle. As a circle-squarer, your mission consists of turning a square into a circle of exactly the same area using only a compass and an unmarked ruler. In 1882 it was proved by mathematicians that it is impossible to do this, which has not stopped many circle-squarers from trying!

Survey by John Langdon. There is a lot going on here. Take your time to figure this one out. Check page 222 to see whether you spotted everything.

A palindrome is a word or sentence that reads the same in either direction. *Able was I ere I saw Elba* is a famous example, which is commonly but mistakenly attributed to Napoleon. Can you find Napoleon in the picture? (See page 222 for the solution if you can't.)

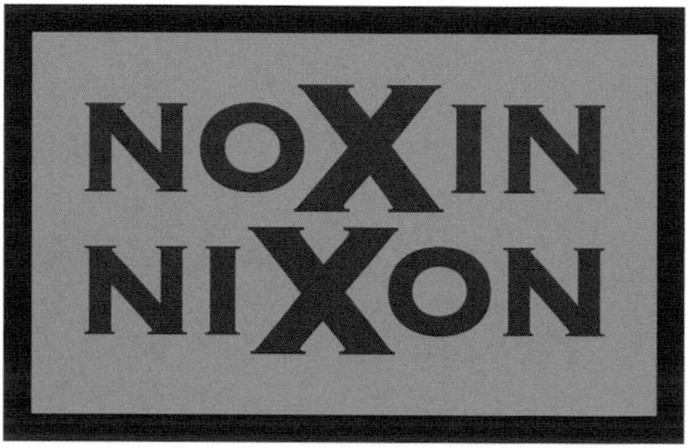

NO X IN NIXON is not only a palindrome but after you push all its letters together also a half-turn ambigram. When you push the letters of the palindrome TOO HOT TO HOOT together you get a wall-reflection ambigram.

The four ambigrams of palindromes on the right highlight the palindromic nature of these words. Here *Malayalam*, a South Indian language, is one of the longest palindrome words. The ambigram of this word is by Nagfa.

malayalam

liveevil

evilolive

Fleetomeremoteelf

According to Plato, the basic building block of the universe is a dodecahedron, a regular figure made up of twelve pentagons. Recent research suggests that our universe may in fact be a giant dodecahedron in which we are trapped. When we try to escape through one of the faces, we re-enter the shape through the opposite face, in the same manner as when playing the computer game *Pacman*. Henry Segerman managed to reshape the twelve letters of the word dodecahedron into an amazing tile, twelve copies of which cover a dodecahedron seamlessly.

DODECAHEDRON

DODECAHEDRON

Take the x- and y-coordinates of a point in the plane and colour it red if

$$\sin[x(\cos y - \cos x)] + \sin x - \sin y < 0$$

otherwise colour it white.
If you do this for all points you get ... lots of bugs!

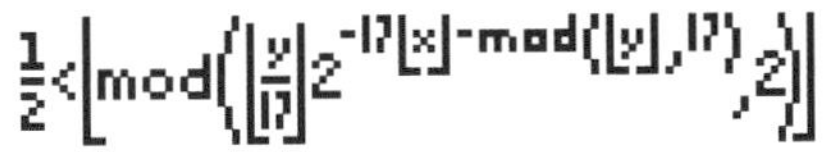

Graphing J. Tupper's formula

$$\frac{1}{2} < \left\lfloor \mathrm{mod}\left(\left\lfloor \frac{y}{17} \right\rfloor 2^{-17\lfloor x \rfloor - \mathrm{mod}(\lfloor y \rfloor, 17)}, 2\right)\right\rfloor$$

does not give bugs as the previous formula, but Tupper's formula itself, as shown above. Amazing!

J.D. Hillberry

Putting It All Together on the left by J. D. Hillberry: 'My two-year-old son was the inspiration and model for this drawing. At this age, he was just beginning to learn about himself and what the world has to offer. I believe that this self-exploration and development continues throughout our lives in our quest to make ourselves whole. When we keep our minds open to new experiences, we are continually "putting it together".'

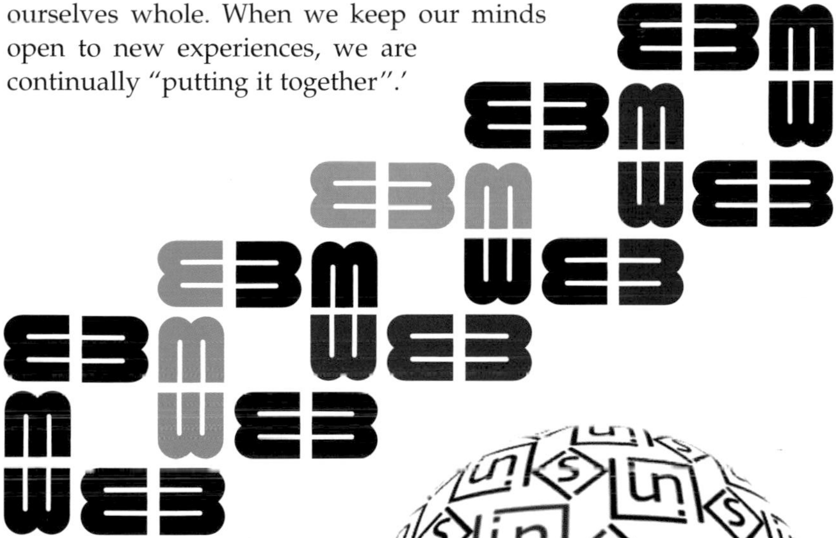

Above, a web of webs made up of one letter only and on the right some links put together by Punya Mishra.

to **ANU**
BOV
CPW
DQX
ERY
FSZ
GTA
HUB
IVC
JWD
KXE
LYF
MZG
NAH
OBI
PCJ
QDK
REL
SFM
TGN
UHO
my **VIP**

This book is dedicated to my wife *Anu* and our two little children. As you can see, there is a 'deeper' reason why Anu is my VIP. If you follow the letter-by-letter transition, you will also come across another curiously relevant three-letter word: hub (which also happens to mean *love* in Arabic).

The nicknames of my two small children are *JuJu* and *DoDo*. While I have been aware of the connection between *Anu* and *VIP* for a long time, the connection between the other three members of my family occurred to me only recently. Note that the words *DoDo* and *JuJu* are the same 'distance' apart as the words *JuJu* and *Pupa*. Of course, this is an incredible coincidence.

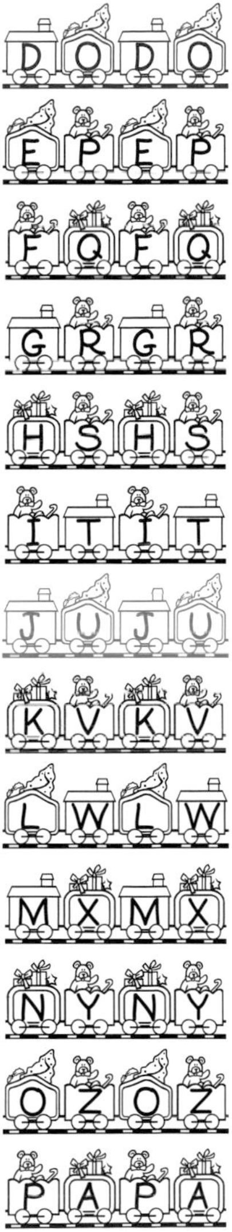

Ambigrams in Action

True or False? In this case the answer is 'both'! Imagine noticing the *False* spray-painted on the pavement on your way to work ...

How do you put ambigrams to work?
Can they actually be useful?
How would you use them in real life?
Find out on the following pages.

... then, on the way back the word has magically turned into the word *True*. How long would it take you to figure out how this magic works? This ambigram, one of my all-time favourites, is by John Langdon.

Two ambigrams by John Langdon in action. The word *transparent* etched into one side of heavy glass and edge-lit from below. This ambigram reads the same viewed from both sides (glasswork by Luc Century, Sanibel, Florida).

Retr + eye + (reflection of Retr in a mirror) = *Retrospect*.

Patrice Hamel's *Réplique no. 5 (1996), Version no. 1 (1998)*. 'Chez l'un , l'autre', Galerie Anton Weller, Paris, 1998. Neon tubes on PVC, placed at right angles to a window, and reflection in the window (photo: Fabrice Fouquet).

Patrice Hamel's *Réplique no. 25 (2002), Version no. 1 (2002)*. 'In Other Words', a personal exhibition in the St-Leger Park Centre of the Arts, Pougues-les-Eaux, 2002. Green neon tubes placed on the ground and reflected in a window (photo: André Morin).

Patrice Hamel's *Réplique no. 22 (2002), Version no. 1 (2002)*. 'Autonommées 2', Ecole des Beaux-Arts, Rouen, 2002. The ambigram is first projected on to the mirror. It becomes visible in the mirror, but also gets reflected on to a wall. Finally, the image on the wall is reflected again in the mirror (photo: Studios Image).

Patrice Hamel's *Réplique no. 8 (1994), Version no. 1 (1998)*. 'Fear of Emptiness', Hôtel Holiday Inn, rue de L'Abbé Grégoire, Paris, 1998. White vinyl letters and reflection in a mirror (photo: Bertrand de Lafargue).

English?

ONEONEONEONEONE
ONEONEONEONEONE

1 2 III IV 5 VI SEVEN 8 nine X 11

A simple ambigram clock face. One of the time ambigram rings contains the word *time* twelve times in each direction and every one of the numbers from 1 to 12 is written as a half-turn ambigram. To make an ambigram clock, photocopy this page, cut out the clock face and paste it on to an actual clock. Other great time ambigram rings can be found in John Langdon's book *Wordplay* and on Punya Mishra's webpage.

In the photo above, the idea was to have the reflection fill in part of reality (part of the *Geometry* ambigram that is printed on the piece of paper and part of my body, which of course is also mirror-symmetric). I noticed too late that the writing on my T-shirt would interfere with the illusion. That is why I am wearing it inside-out.

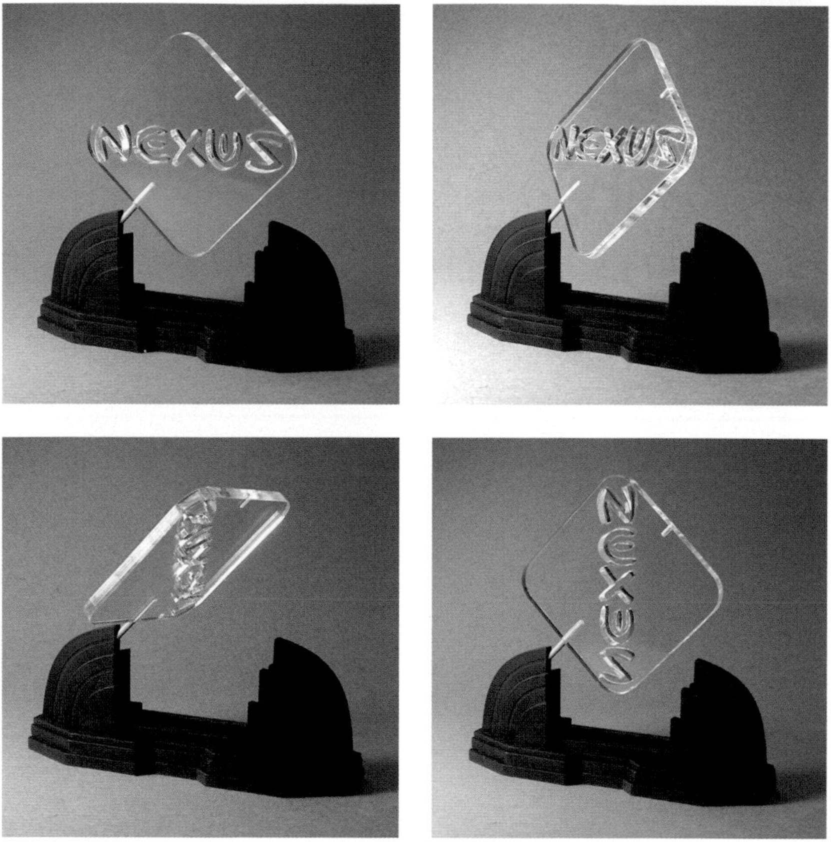

Nexus by Tom Banwell is the only ambigram of its kind in this book. Although it may look like a quarter-turn ambigram at first sight, it is not. It is also possible to access the second reading of this ambigram using a mirror. Can you see how? (See page 222 for the solution.)

Live read backwards is *evil*. Here Tom Banwell takes this idea two steps further. This is a photo of a curled-up strip of leather from which letters have been carved with a laser cutter.

The picture above is simply the mirror image of the picture on the left, but what a difference.

TATTOO

From *BODY TYPE: Intimate Messages Etched in Flesh* by Ina Saltz. The ambigrams are *Philosophy/Art & Science* and *Angels & Demons* by John Langdon.

TATTOO

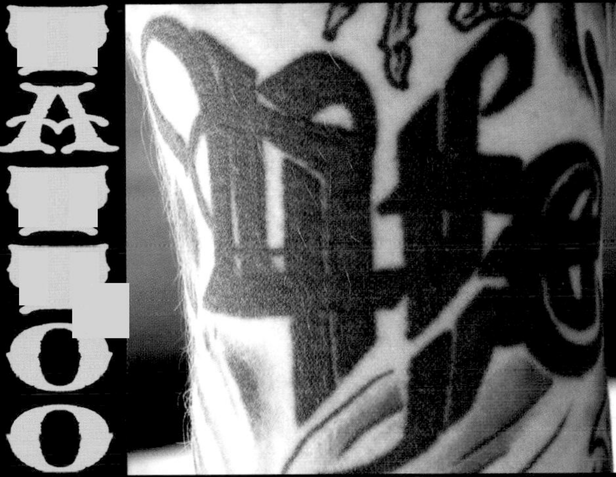

From the same book *Life/Death*, a very popular ambigram tattoo in action.

Some of Mark Palmer's tattoo designs etched in skin: *faith, love, michele/gareth, live/life, agape.*

ART CAR
Connecticut
ART·MKT
Constitution State

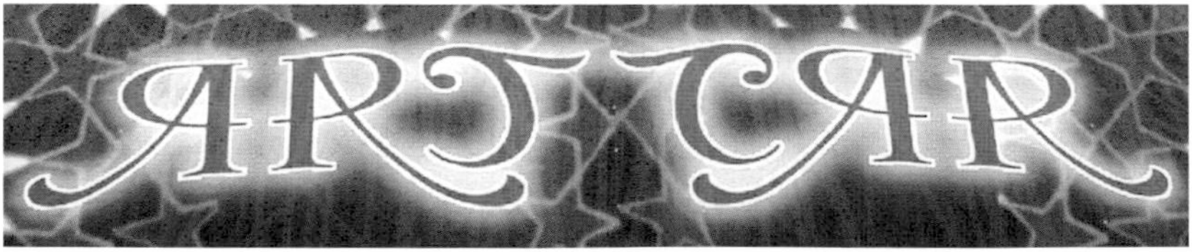
ART CAR

PUZZLING PROBLEMS

Scott Kim's mirror-symmetric *Art Car* ambigram commissioned by *Artists' Market*, Norwalk, CT (www.artistsmarket.com). The two photos may appear to be identical at first glance. However, this is not the case – one is a photo of the car and one is the mirror image of this photo. Which is which? (See page 222 for the solution.)

Put the decimals in order

What symbol follows the triangle?

(See page 223 for the solutions.)

Solve two Sudoku puzzles in one

4		7				5		9
		2	9			3		8
				7	8			
		8	5			2		3
			2		3			
2		5			7	8		
			7	3				
8		1			2	7		
		6				4		5

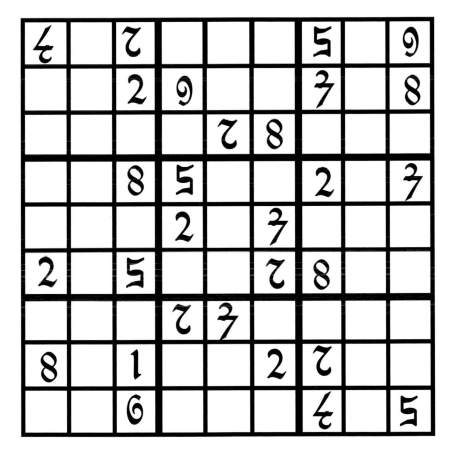

Use the special ways to write the decimals on the left to simultaneously solve this Sudoku puzzle and the one you arrive at by turning it upside-down.

Correcting an incorrect sum

340
437
74813

43373414

Decode this secret message

umop ap!sdn

(See page 224 for the solutions.)

BY LOOKING AT IT
IN A MIRROR

Solve the cryptoambigram ...

... by John Langdon which fuses the two given names of a married couple.

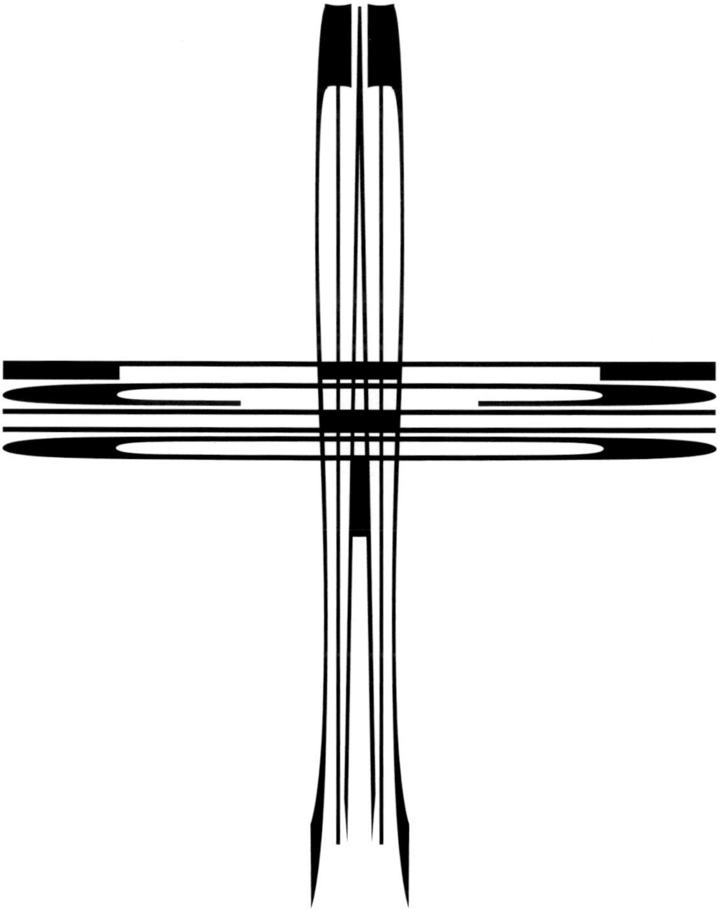

Why is this drawing called *Echo Star*?

(See pages 224–5 for the solutions.)

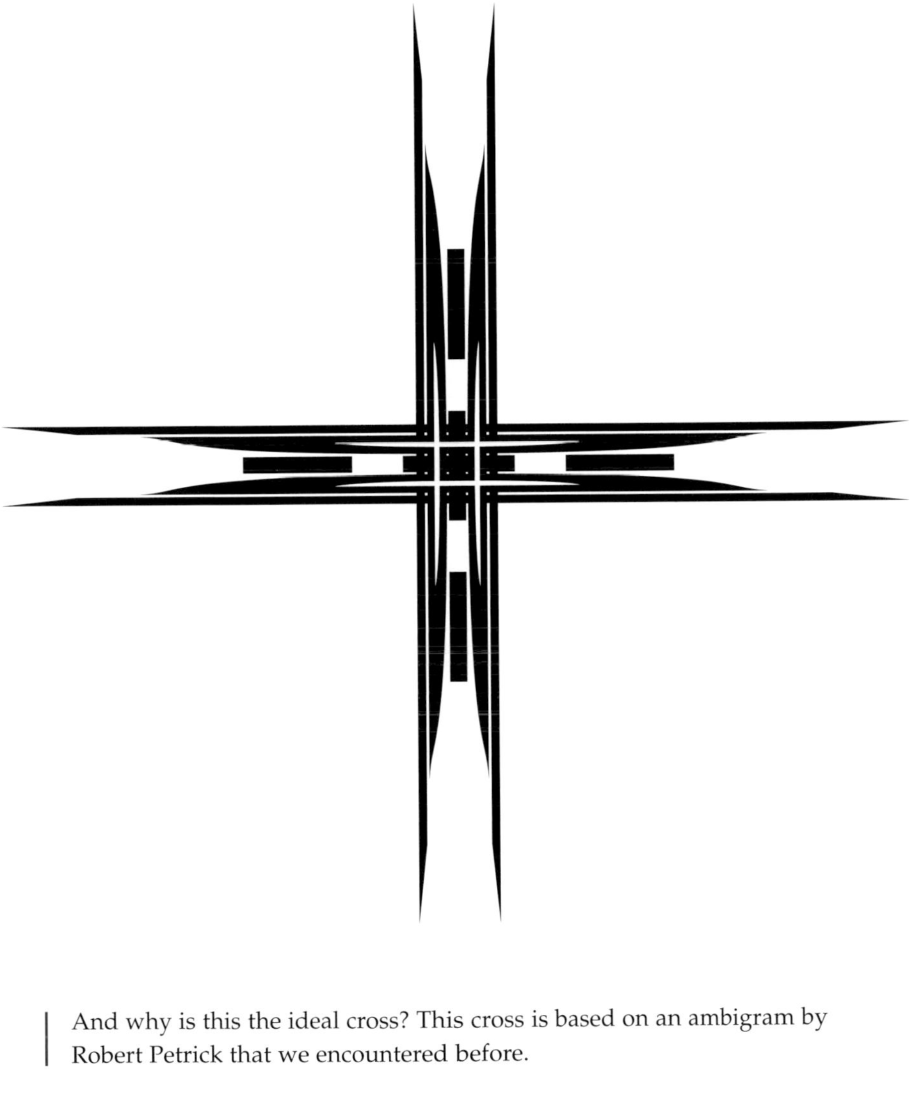

And why is this the ideal cross? This cross is based on an ambigram by Robert Petrick that we encountered before.

How many presents?

On the sixth day of Christmas,
my true love sent to me
Six Geese a-laying,
Five golden Rings,
Four calling Birds,
Three French Hens,
Two turtle Doves,
And a Partridge in a pear tree.

On the 6th day of Christmas you get 1+2+3+4+5+6 presents. A smart way to calculate how many presents you get on that day is to note that the rectangle on the right is made up of twice as many circles as there are presents. Therefore you get 7 (circles wide) x 6 (circles tall)/2 = 21 presents. How many presents do you get on the 12th day of Christmas? And what about the 1,000th day of Christmas? (See page 225 for the solutions.)

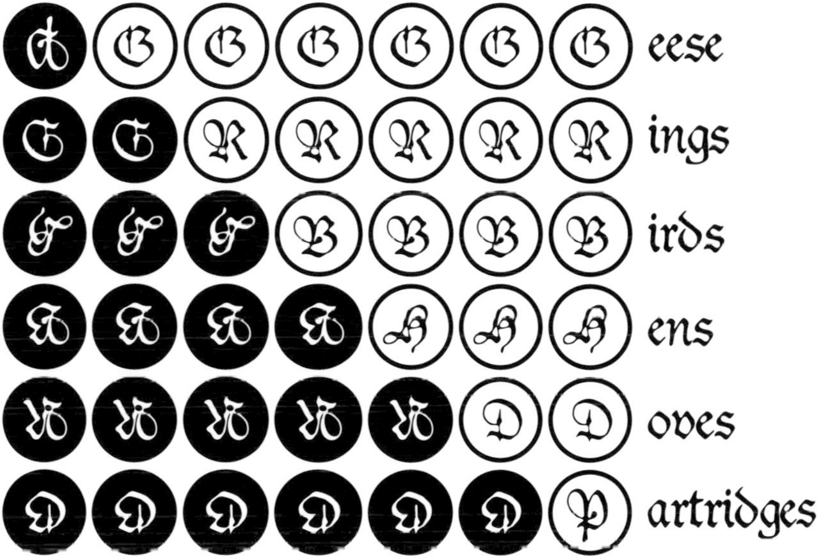
eese
ings
irds
ens
oves
artridges

algebra

Why

is

smiles

the

longest

ambigram?

Looking at

CARBON DIOXIDE

through the stem

of a wine glass

you see

CARBON DIOXIDE

Why does only

one of the words

stand on its head?

(See pages 225–6 for the solutions.)

MELENCOLIA I

Magic Squares

16	3	2	13
5	10	11	8
9	6	7	12
4	15	14	1

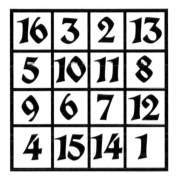

In a magic square like the one in Dürer's engraving *Melencolia I* all rows and columns add up to the same number (in this famous example 34). Google this square to find out about its other amazing features: it contains all the numbers from 1 to 16, the entries 15 and 14 in the last line combine into the year 1514 in which the engraving was made, etc.

96	11	89	68
88	69	91	16
61	86	18	99
19	98	66	81

five	twenty-two	eighteen
twenty-eight	fifteen	two
twelve	eight	twenty-five

1111	8818	8881	1188
8188	1881	1818	8111
1888	8181	8118	1811
8811	1118	1181	8888

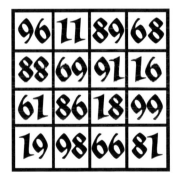

Unlike the Dürer square, these last three number squares are magic in at least two different ways each. Can you figure out how? For some really surprising answers, see pages 226–7.

The designs on these two pages are some of Scott Kim's *Double Talk* puzzles. Each design is actually half of a word. To create the whole words, make two copies of this page and slide one on top of the other until the two copies of a particular design make a whole word. Hold the pages up to the light to see through the paper. You may have to turn or flip the page. No folding allowed.

HOTS

For instance, the first design makes the word 'mirror' if you flip one of the copies to look through the back. Can you figure out what the other words say? The solutions are on page 228. If you can do these by just looking at this page, you are a born ambigrammist.

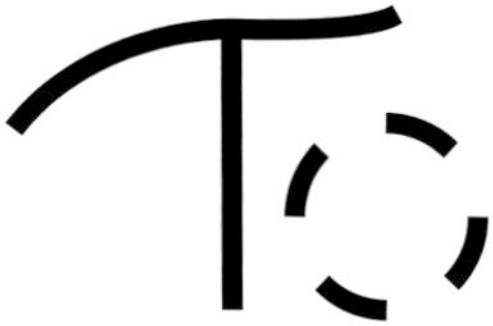

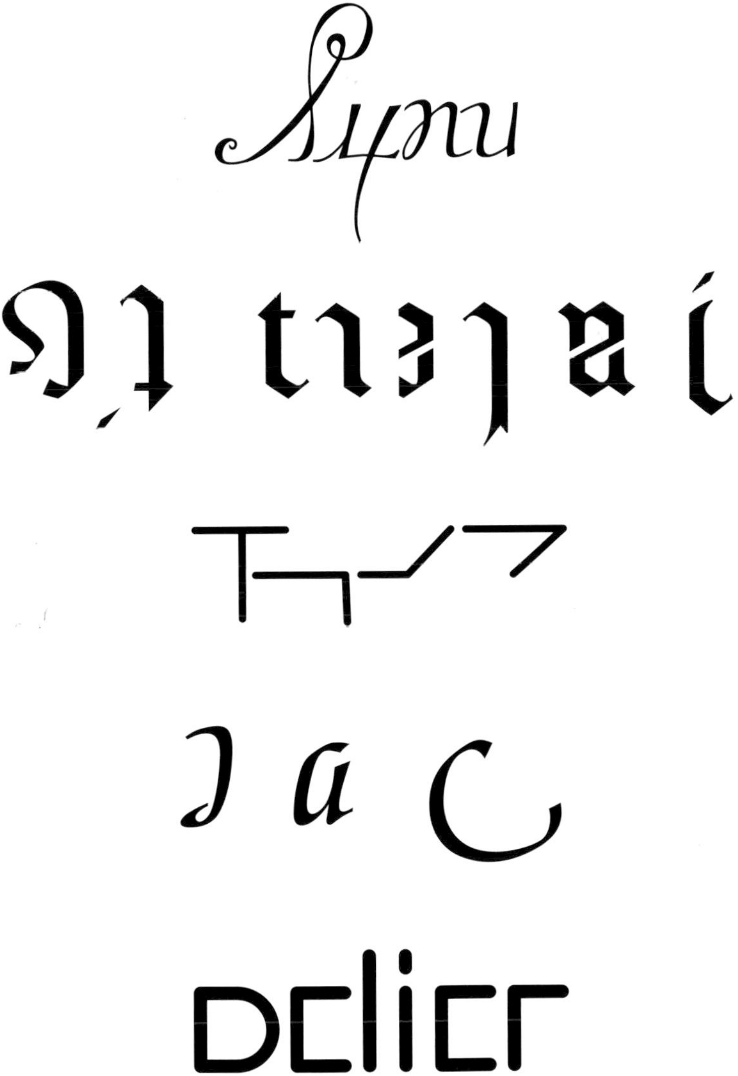

Four different letter shapes that read as different letters depending on how you turn and reflect them. Write a three-letter word starting with *m* using only the first shape, a six-letter word starting with *b* using the second shape (tricky!),

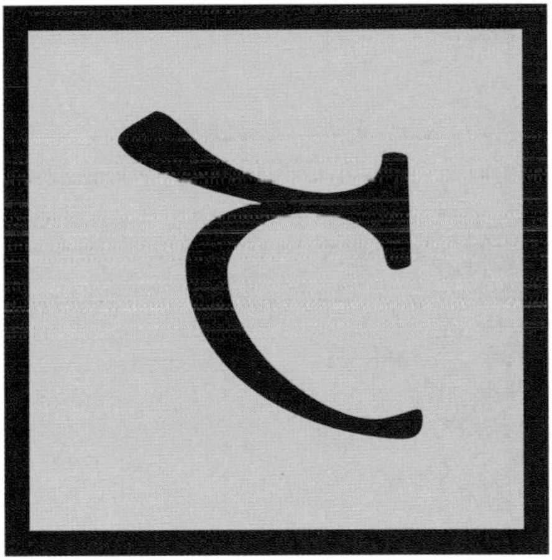

a five-letter word starting with *s* using the third shape, and a five-letter word starting with *t* using the last shape. The two shapes on this page are by Tom Banwell. For the answers, see page 229.

DIY

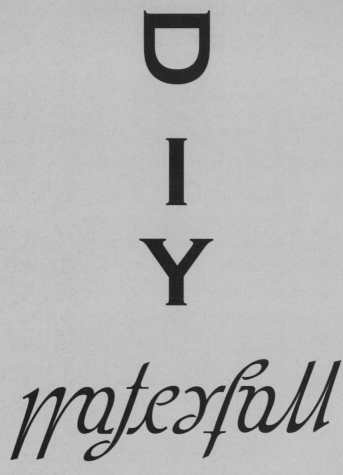

A very readable and attractive ambigram of the word *waterfall*. One problem with this ambigram is that it does not reflect the meaning of the word – it is hard to imagine an upside-down waterfall, unless it is an Escher waterfall. A wall-reflection ambigram of the word would work much better. You can find such an ambigram in John Langdon's *Wordplay*.

Do It Yourself!

What constitutes a good ambigram?

Most ambigram artists would agree that a good ambigram should be readable, attractive and ideally reflect some of the meaning of the word it represents. Of course, it is up to the individual to decide what looks good and what does not. While a graphic designer may be mostly interested in readability and calligraphic beauty, a puzzle fan may prefer an ambigram that is more of a puzzle that needs to be figured out. Whatever your personal notion of a good ambigram may be, I think it is safe to say that it is not possible to find a good ambigram for every word.

So how do you go about finding and designing good ambigrams? There are a lot of important issues here. First, designing ambigrams is not an exact science and it will take a considerable effort on your part if you aim to become any good at it. Second, although there is a lot of trial and error involved in the design of ambigrams, there are a number of rules and guiding principles that can greatly facilitate matters.

A very readable and quite attractive ambigram of Escher's name. Given that many of the drawings of this famous Dutch graphic artist have an ambiguous feel to them, it seems very appropriate to turn his name into an ambigram.

To get you started I will describe two semi-automatic methods for designing half-turn ambigrams. Although the two techniques will allow you to find rough ambigrams for any word, hardly any ambigram created with only one of these techniques will look attractive. A creative mix of both techniques is needed to create good ambigrams. Rather than trying to pin down exactly what I mean by this vague statement, I recommend that you first read this chapter and then study various good ambigrams, figuring out in every single case to what extent these techniques played a role in their creation.

An ambigram of the word *snake*. Quite attractive but not very readable.

This chapter also contains a list of rules for designing ambigrams that I have found to be most helpful. Although I will focus on the design of half-turn ambigrams, many of the rules also apply to other types of ambigrams. Finally, both John Langdon's *Wordplay* and Scott Kim's *Inversions* include great introductions to the art of making ambigrams.

The Letter-by-Letter Technique

David Holt's website *Ambigram.Matic.Com* features a computer program which on input of any word produces a half-turn ambigram of this word. This ambigram generator uses a 26x26 table of letter shapes whose entry number *m* in row *n* resembles the *m*th letter of the alphabet when looked at right side up and resembles the *n*th letter upside-down. The table below is a table similar to, and partly based on, the table used by the ambigram generator.

The letter-by-letter ambigram of a word starts with the letter shape

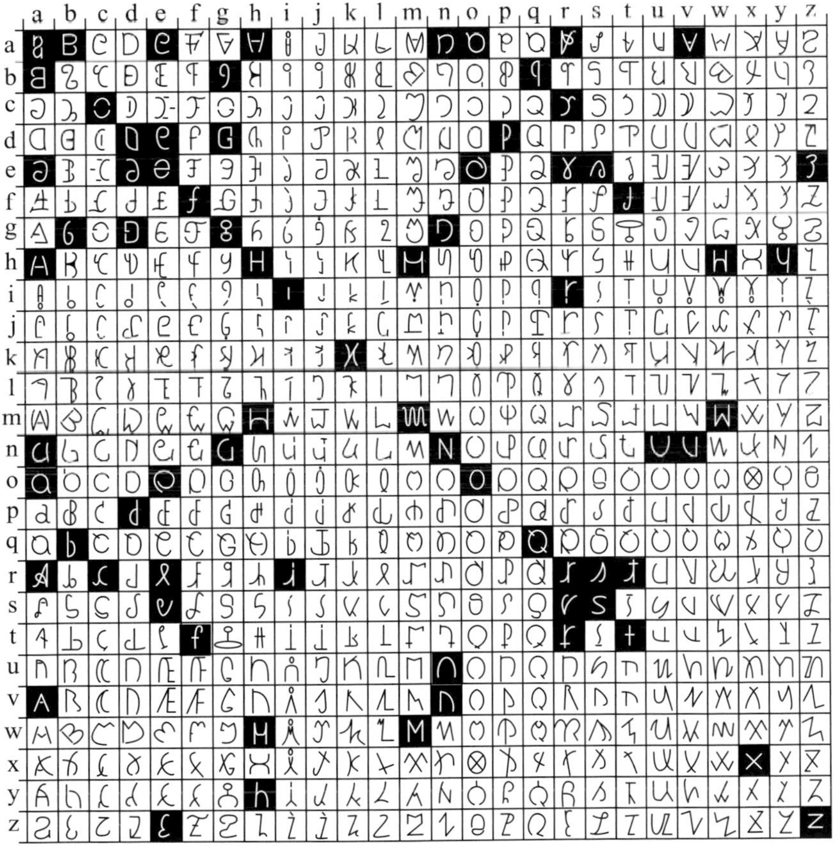

that corresponds to the first and last letter of the word, followed by the letter shape that corresponds to the second and penultimate letter of the word, etc. Note that using this technique also allows you to merge any two words with the same number of letters into an ambigram. Sounds easy: so what's the catch?

Usually, the ambigrams produced by this letter-by-letter technique will be very rough, unreadable and look fairly unattractive. Nevertheless, it is a fun technique to play with and provides you with a first draft of an ambigram which can then be refined. In fact, most successful ambigrams are based on letters in the word they represent that naturally turn into themselves or other letters in the word when you rotate them. Many of the most useful letter inversions are present in the table and I have highlighted some of my favourites among them.

The half-turn ambigram of Escher's name generated by the letter-by-letter technique. The *e/r* and *s/e* letter inversions in this ambigram are very useful. It is easy to turn this letter-by-letter ambigram into the nice Escher ambigram on page 173.

Using the letter-by-letter technique allows you to merge any two words with the same number of letters. Above you can see *art* and *tao*.

The Stroke-by-Stroke Technique for Half-Turn Ambigrams

In the simple font below, every letter contains one, two or three vertical strokes. The distance between neighbouring vertical strokes is the same for all letters. It is easy to turn the word *ram* into an ambigram using the stroke-by-stroke technique.

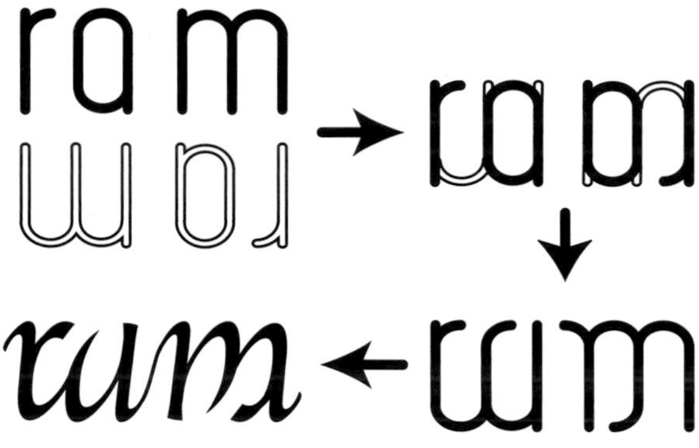

1 Write the word you want to turn into an ambigram using our special font.

2 Superimpose the word and its rotated image.

3 Make minor adjustments to arrive at a working ambigram.

4 Finally, have a go at writing the ambigram in calligraphic letters.

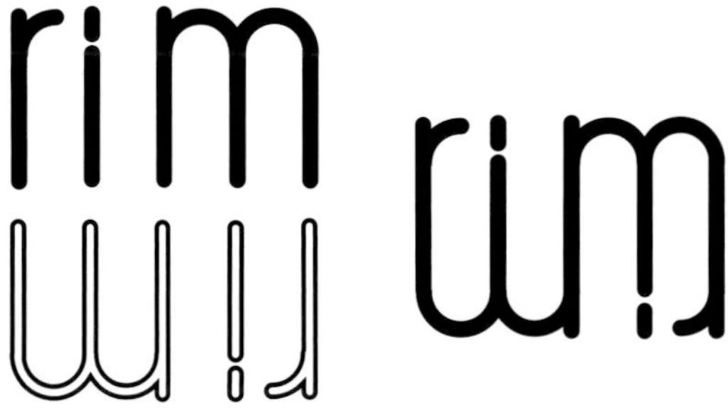

Letters that are open-ended at the bottom such as *f*, *i*, *l*, *m*, *n* and *r* merge particularly well with letters of the same type and can facilitate the tricky Step 3. For example, the word *rim* consist of three of those letters and no adjustments need to be made in Step 3.

Mixing the Stroke-by-Stroke and Letter-by-Letter Techniques

In designing a good ambigram for the word *ambigram,* mix the stroke-by-stroke and the letter-by-letter techniques. Note that the word *big* written in our special font is an almost natural half-turn ambigram, almost exactly in the middle of our word.

1 Align the word *ambigram* and its rotated image such that the word *big* and its rotated image are positioned one on top of the other.

2 Superimpose our word and its rotated image, and make minor adjustments to arrive at the ambigram on the right.

3 Use a computer drawing package to render this ambigram in calligraphic letters. The flourish was added to conceal the additional stroke in front of the leading letter *a* of our ambigram.

The Rules

Rule 1: A good ambigram should be readable (or at least decipherable) and attractive.

Rule 2: Do not compromise on symmetry. For example, if you are designing a half-turn ambigram, don't be satisfied with anything that does not have the required rotational symmetry.

The Dos and Don'ts

1: *Follow the rules but don't be afraid to cheat (a little).* Break as few rules as possible. Try not to mix upper-case with lower-case letters and letters that seem to belong to different fonts. Having said all this it is sometimes necessary to cheat a little. For example, certain functional parts of letters sometimes need to be turned into flourishes. Still, if you have to cheat, try to make it look as natural as possible.

2 *(for beginners): Just do it.* Try to find half-turn ambigrams of some words that are important to you. Names of friends and family are a good starting point. Keep these special words in mind while browsing through this and other books on ambigrams. See whether you can figure out some of the rules that make ambigrams work and apply them to your own problem. As with most activities that involve a mix of logic, craftsmanship and artistic expression, the only way to get good at designing ambigrams is to create lots of them and to study many examples.

3: *Be flexible.* Rather than focusing on a particular word, try to work with a certain theme in mind. If a word refuses to be turned into an ambigram, then try a short form of a first name, or add initials to a last name; use the plural form instead of the singular form.

4: *If it's no good, throw it away and start again!*

In designing the ambigram of the word *ambigram* I had to cheat a little bit by adding a curve that acts as a flourish on the left side *a* while its rotated image is an essential part of the last letter *m*. There is also a superfluous *i* dot. However, since these additional features look quite natural and allowed me to avoid breaking any symmetries, I don't have any problems with tricks such as these. Note also that all the letters in this ambigram seem to belong to one font and that only lower-case letters were used.

Sometimes short versions of names are easier to turn into ambigrams than full names. Sometimes long versions of names give better results than their short forms. Experiment with different versions if you are after an ambigram of a particular name.

Maybe you cannot think of any good way to turn the word *star* into an ambigram. Try *stars* instead. On the other hand, you may be stuck trying to tame *stars* and turning the singular star into an ambigram may come more naturally to you.

Design Protocol

My favourite ambigrams are half-turn ambigrams. If some other form of ambigram is suggested by a word or if nothing else works, I will start looking for other ways to turn a given word into an ambigram. As before, I will focus on my protocol for designing my favourite type of ambigram.

1 Write the word you want to turn into an ambigram on a piece of paper. Also write it upside-down (if you can't picture this in your mind).

2 Identify the ambigrammatic skeleton of the word: that is, the letters that naturally turn into themselves or other letters in the word. Usually a word remains readable if you delete a couple of letters from it. Therefore it is more likely that a word can be turned into a readable ambigram if it contains a large ambi-skeleton. If you find a natural ambi-skeleton within a word you can usually get away with a more daring approach when you flesh out this skeleton into a fully fledged ambigram.

3 Decide whether this skeleton can be turned into a standard ambigram of the word or some closely related word using a mix of the letter-by-letter, the stroke-by-stroke and the cannot-be-described-in-words techniques.

4 If this is not possible, check whether a chain or ring ambigram is possible.

5 Home in on the ideal ambigram by scribbling a couple of versions on a piece of paper until the overall shape of the ambigram looks about right.

6 Use a computer drawing package such as Adobe Illustrator or Macromedia Freehand to design a professional-looking ambigram with an exact symmetry.

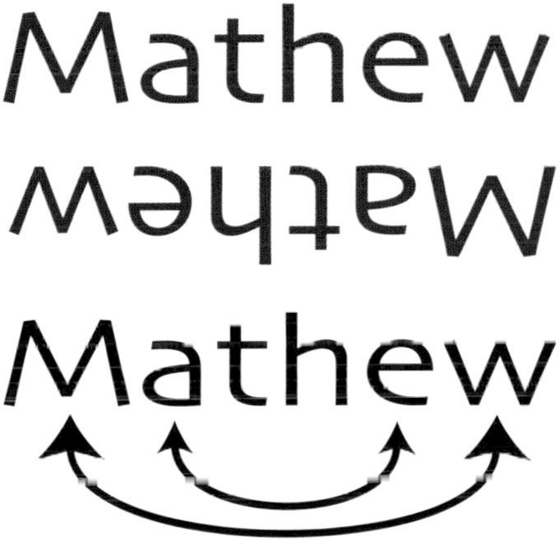

The ambigrammatic skeleton of a word consists of the letters that naturally turn into themselves or other letters in the word. In this example the skeleton consists of almost all the letters *(m, a, e, w)* in the word. A large ambi-skeleton such as this makes the design of the ambigram of the name *Mathew* into an easy task. (See overleaf for the final ambigram.)

This name's ambi-skeleton is visible only to those among us who are used to stroke-by-stroke juggling. If you are, you will see immediately that the *M* turns naturally into *t* and *y* and how the letters *a* and *r* can be fused naturally.

Drawing packages give you complete control over the design process by providing tools that allow you to draw smooth curves of any shape, copy and dissect existing shapes, rotate objects, apply calligraphic tools to curves and, most importantly, fiddle with any aspect of a design until you are really happy with it.

Computer Design

I use a number of different techniques for designing ambigrams on a computer. All letters in a good font or ambigram usually look very similar. This is usually due to the fact that there is a basic set of curves or shapes from which all letters contained in the font or ambigram can be assembled. It is possible to convert professionally designed fonts on your computer into graphic objects, which can then be manipulated just like any object created from scratch. Very often it is possible to dissect different letters contained in one font into a set of basic shapes for the ambigram under consideration. For example, the simple ambigram of the name *Mathew* is based on a professionally designed font. I dissected and reassembled the letters *a*, *w*, *t* and *h* in this font to make up this ambigram.

The letters in this basic alphabet are made up of only two different types of curves: vertical strokes and quarter circles. Using only a small number of common basic curves in the design of the letters in an ambigram guarantees that all the letters will look alike.

The ambigram of the word *ambigram* based on the same set of basic curves.

This ambigram is based on a professionally designed font.

The computer drawing package Adobe Illustrator is my weapon of choice when it comes to designing ambigrams. These two reflection ambigrams of the word *adobe* were created from existing fonts using Adobe Illustrator.

If you want to design an ambigram of a word from scratch, start by fiddling one of the tricky letters or letter combinations in the word into the shape you want it in (as a collection of curves), then dissect the members of the resulting set into a basic set of curves for the remaining letters of your ambigram. Once you are satisfied with the overall shape of your ambigram, you can add some calligraphic flourishes to it. As a first approximation I recommend playing with the calligraphic tools that come with most drawing packages, and then refining their output by hand.

Of course, if you are prepared to learn more about calligraphy and font design, you will be able to further improve your results. On the following two pages some of the technical details of ambigram design on a computer are dealt with. I assume some familiarity with drawing packages such as Adobe Illustrator. Most of the Illustrator commands mentioned have counterparts in other vector graphics drawing packages.

Five Important Tools in Adobe Illustrator

The **Rotate Tool** rotates objects around a fixed point. Use it to create perfect half-turn ambigrams.

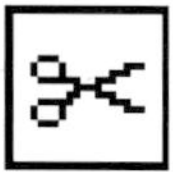

The **Scissors Tool** splits paths. Use it to dissect and recycle letters from existing fonts.

The **Pen Tool** draws curves of any shape. Use it to create the first computer draft of your ambigram.

The **Reflect Tool** flips objects over a fixed axis. Use it to create perfect mirror ambigrams.

The **Direct Selection Tool** is the main fiddle-everything-into-shape tool in Illustrator.

Making Ambigrams from Existing Fonts in Adobe Illustrator (CS2)

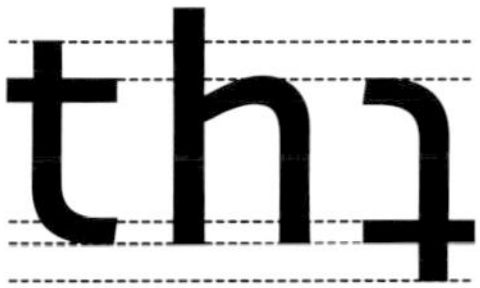

Constructing the *th* in the middle of the *Mathew* ambigram: start by aligning the letters to be used.

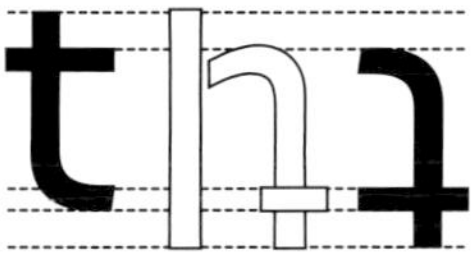

Cut the *h* in two, add a horizontal stroke and extend/contract the vertical strokes.

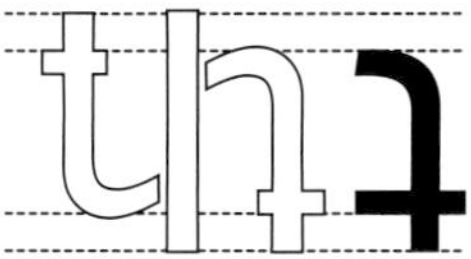

Clean up using the **Unite** command, make a copy of the right part of the *h* and paste it in on the left.

1 Decide which of the fonts present on your computer contains a sufficient number of letters that can be dissected and reassembled into the letters of your ambigram.

2 Type all the letters that you want to use in Illustrator.

3 Select all letters with the **Selection Tool** and select **Expand** from the **Object** menu. This turns the letters into vector graphics objects.

4 Use the **Scissors Tool** to dissect and reassemble the letters into something that closely resembles the right half or the left half of the ambigram you have in mind. Usually, you end up with several pieces that overlap each other. It is now time to clean up and make every connected letter combination on the screen into a single object whose contour lines can be easily manipulated. This is done in the next step.

5 Select everything on the screen, bring up the Pathfinder palette by selecting **Pathfinder** under the **Windows** menu, press the **Unite** button and hit **Expand**.

6 Fiddle the resulting letters into the shape you want them in using the **Direct Selection Tool**.

7 Use the **Rotate Tool** to create an exact rotated copy of the first half of your ambigram and combine the two halves into the full ambigram.

Calligraphic Ambigrams from Scratch in Adobe Illustrator

1 Draw the first letter of the ambigram you have in mind using the **Pen Tool** and fiddle it into shape using the **Direct Selection Tool**. At regular intervals during the design process turn whatever you have drawn so far on its head using the **Rotation Tool**. Continue to work on the upside-down design for a while before you turn it right side up again.

2 Design all the other letters in one-half of your ambigram based mostly on strokes that are already present in the first letter.

3 Use the **Rotate Tool** to create an exact rotated image of the first half of your ambigram and combine the two halves into the full ambigram.

4 Select your whole design and apply a calligraphic stroke to it via the **Brushes** palette. The resulting calligraphic rendering is usually somewhat rough and needs to be cleaned up a bit. To do this first select everything and outline the strokes in your design using **Expand Appearance** in the **Object** menu. You can now play with the outlines until you are happy with your ambigram.

To render the *ram* ambigram in calligraphic script, first draw the letter *a*.

Then compose the remaining letters from strokes in *a*.

Render the ambigram in rough calligraphic script using the **Brushes** palette.

Clean up using a combination of **Pathfinder** tools. Finally, apply the finishing touches by hand.

Some More Words of Wisdom on Designing Ambigrams from the Ambigram Masters Scott Kim and John Langdon

Scott Kim

'The alphabet was not designed with inversions (ambigrams) in mind … Letters can be stretched in many different dimensions and remain legible. Without this flexibility inversions would not be possible.'

'What usually happens is that a couple of letters will invert easily but the rest stubbornly refuse to follow the pattern. This is where imagination comes in.'

'One of the most useful techniques to master is letter regrouping.'
[This is what happens naturally when we apply the stroke-by-stroke technique.]

'First choose a word to work on. I enjoy choosing words that mean something special to me … Finding a solution requires imagination, persistence and faith that a solution just might lie waiting to be discovered.'

'Almost anything with a dot on it can serve as an i.'

'The best way to incorporate an awkward letter shape is to find a style in which it appears natural ... I cannot stress enough how powerfully legibility and overall coherence are enhanced by a consistent style.'

John Langdon

'As a professional lettering artist, I have two primary requirements of an ambigram: it should be readable and it should be attractive. In addition, I think that an ambigram reaches its greatest potential when it provokes thought beyond a mere appreciation of its symmetry – when there is a resonant relationship between the word, its meaning and its "ambigraphic" representation.'

'If a word is likely to work as an ambigram, it almost always depends on some letters being natural reverses of either themselves or other letters. These provide support for the letters that require more distortion and manipulation and might, out of context, be difficult to read.'

'Designing an ambigram is not like designing a typeface. In the design of a typeface, each letter must perform well … on either side of every other letter in the alphabet. I call this an "open system". An ambigram is a "closed system". The letters that are drawn for one specific ambigram may not be recognizable outside the context of that ambigram.'

'It's a handy little secret that if a word resists my attempts to make an ambigram out of it, then a gothic blackletter style (often incorrectly referred to as "Old English") is often a successful last resort. The style is somewhat familiar to anyone who's ever seen the masthead of a newspaper, the church bulletin, or certain *Grateful Dead* or heavy-metal album covers, and yet many of the individual letters, and parts of letters, are quite unorthodox in comparison to most of the typestyles we regularly see. This combination of familiarity and unfamiliarity allows for significant letter manipulation.'

Meet the Artists

In this chapter you have the opportunity to learn more about the various artists who have contributed to this book. We start out with four of the pioneers of the art of ambigrams, John Langdon, Scott Kim, Douglas Hofstadter and Robert Petrick, and continue from there.

John Langdon

John Langdon does just about everything that can be done with words; he is a logo designer and custom typography specialist, a lettering artist and a writer. He teaches in the Graphic Design programme at Drexel University in Philadelphia and has been an independent designer since 1977. His logo clients range from Aerosmith to the Rehabilitation Hospitals of America, and his designs have won numerous awards; they have also been shown in *U&lc*, *Print*, *American Corporate Identity* and *Letter Arts Review*.

John's passions for language, illusion and ambiguity are best realized in his unique approach to the design of ambigrams which he pioneered in the early 1970s, trying to do with words what Dalí and Escher had done with images. John's ambigrams form the basis for his 1992 book, *Wordplay*. A second edition was published in November 2005. His best-known work is the group of ambigrams he created for Dan Brown's bestselling novel, *Angels & Demons*. John's approach to the development of ambigrams is very closely intertwined with his Taoist philosophy and principles of traditional physics. His aesthetic

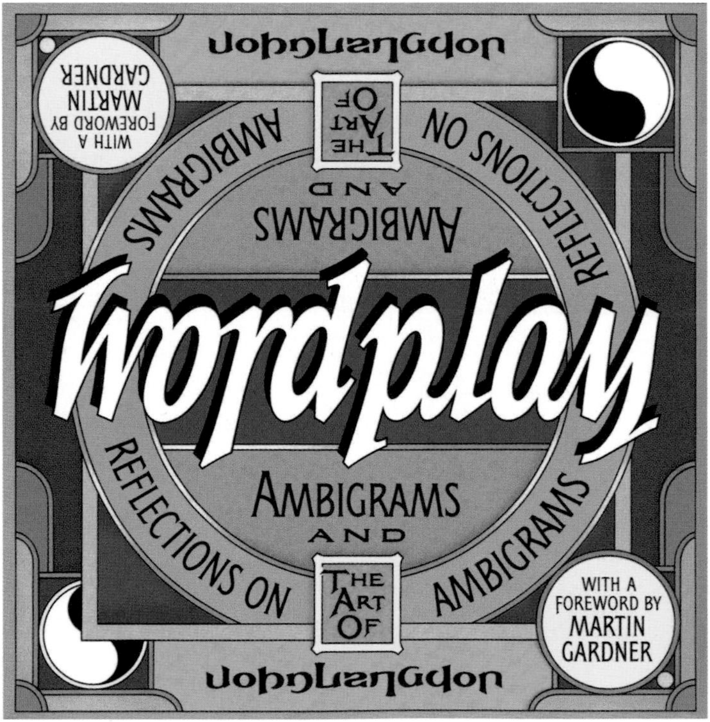

standards for his ambigrams are greatly influenced by his background in conventional and classic typography, and his career in corporate logo design.

Since 1995, John has taken his wordworks to canvas. His paintings still involve symmetry and illusion, a bit of philosophy and a few puns thrown in for good measure.

The cover of John's 1992 edition of *Wordplay* and two of his ambigrams that appeared in Dan Brown's *Angels & Demons*: an ambigram of the title of the book and on the previous page, the famous *Earth-Air-Fire-Water* diamond. The fact that the hero of the novel is called Langdon is also not a coincidence. John's website www.johnlangdon.net is a must-visit for every ambigram lover.

SCOTT KIM

Scott Kim is a puzzle designer and graphic designer with a background in music, mathematics and computer science from Stanford University. His creations include a monthly puzzle column in *Discover* magazine, an annual page-a-day Brainteasers calendar, puzzles for computer games such as Bejeweled and Collapse, and the puzzle toy Railroad Rush Hour from ThinkFun. In 2006 he joined his wife Amy Jo Kim to create Shufflebrain, which designs games and social architecture for online services.

In 1975 he took his first graphic design class and fell in love with lettering, creating his first ambigram. His lettering work first appeared in *Omni* magazine in 1979, then in his book *Inversions*, published in 1981. His lettering work includes logos for Ford Aerospace and Silicon Graphics, as well as animated titles for video. Not content to stick with conventional ambigrams, Scott is constantly inventing new types of lettering, such as bilingual ambigrams, animated ambigrams and interactive ambigram games.

Scott's passion for integrating the arts into mathematics education led him to create books and posters about symmetry for maths teachers, an interactive course in visual thinking for engineers, and stage performances about mathematics in collaboration with the Dr Schaffer and Mr Stern Dance Ensemble. He is currently working on books and games that use puzzles to teach mathematics.

On the right, *teach/learn* and *Inversions/Scott Kim*, the title of Scott's book and the name of its author fused into a half-turn ambigram. Visit Scott's website www.scottkim.com for many more examples of his ambigrams, games and puzzles.

Inversions

Scott Kim

Douglas Hofstadter

Many people know Doug Hofstadter as the author of the Pulitzer Prize-winning book *Gödel, Escher, Bach: An Eternal Golden Braid*. Around 1962, his friend Peter Jones rediscovered the art of writing names and words in either a rotational or a mirror-symmetric fashion, and they made a few dozen such designs together. A decade later, Doug met Scott Kim and, inspired by Scott's designs, took up the idea again. In 1983, seeking a word for the ambiguous calligraphic designs that he, Scott and a small coterie of friends were making, he suggested the term 'ambigram'; the word seemed to appeal to the group, and it stuck. Over the course of a decade, Doug produced a few thousand ambigrams, and in so doing developed an idiosyncratic and recognizable style.

In 1987, his book *Ambigrammi*, featuring hundreds of his ambigrams, was published in Italy.

Doug never uses a computer in any way, always creating his work first in pencil and then in felt-tip pen. He believes that the first and foremost goal in creating ambigrams is instant, effortless legibility with a minimum of unexplained shapes.

In his 'other' life, Doug is a professor of cognitive science at Indiana University, where, with his graduate students, he studies many aspects of the mind, including analogy-making, error-making, creativity and consciousness.

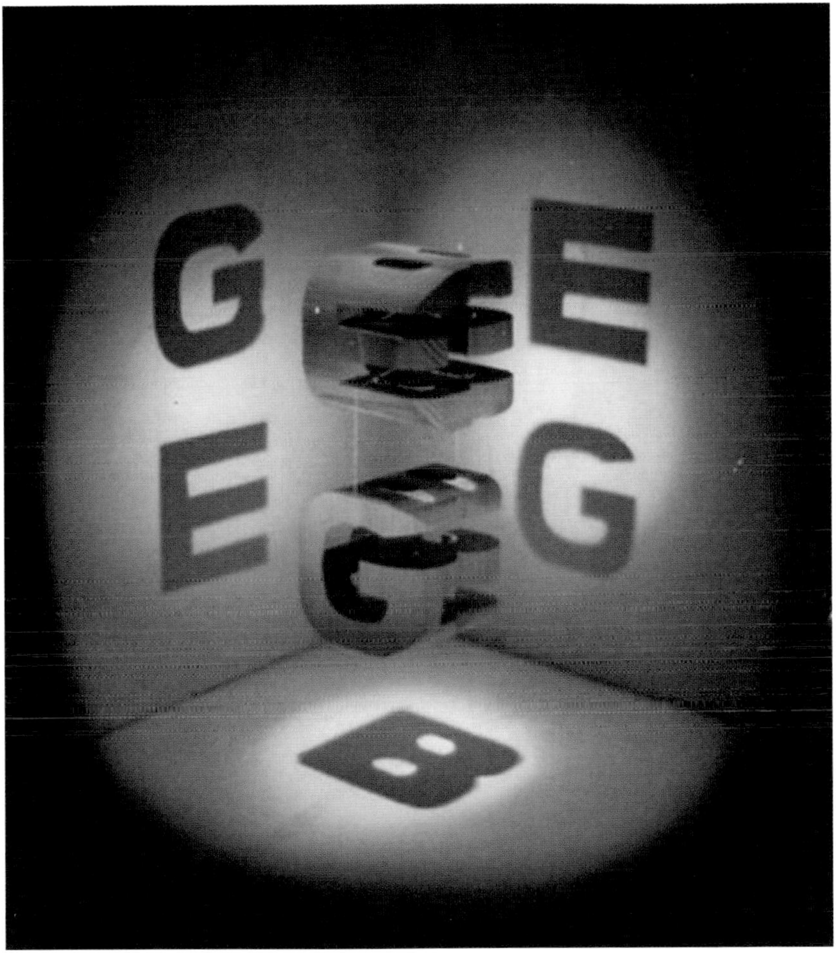

The title illustration of Doug's famous book *Gödel, Escher, Bach* shows two blocks of wood each of which spell out the letters GEB as shadows in different directions.

ROBERT PETRICK

Robert Petrick is a graphic designer, lettering artist and painter. His interest in ambigrams began in the early 1970s, when he started working with and became friends with John Langdon. They were both influenced by the period's dynamic design world, particularly the design group of Herb Lubalin. In 1975 Robert produced the perfectly symmetrical logo *Angel* for the now defunct 'Casablanca Records'. He went to a concert where the group was performing and they loved it. It was first used by the band in 1976, and then on five different albums over the next ten years. More of Robert's ambigrams can be found at www.cafepress.com/rwp2006 and members.aol.com/robertpetrick.

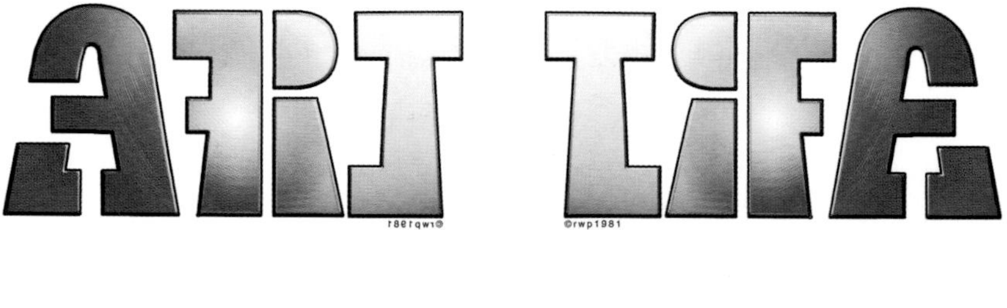

organic, art is life, magic,
love and peace, angel

Roberto & Renato Fernandez

Roberto and Renato Fernandez are twins who both studied industrial design and advertising, and are currently art directors for two of the largest advertising agencies in Brazil: Roberto for JWT Brasil and and Renato for Almap. Both have won awards for their work at the major international advertising festivals. Some of their ambigram-related award-winning work can be admired on this page; for more examples see www.robertofernandez.com.br and www.renatofernandez.com.

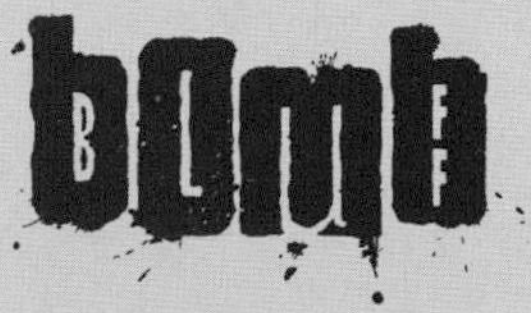

The illustrations shown here were part of two political campaigns for the Brazilian magazine *Veja* entitled 'Get both sides' and deal with current-affairs issues. The faces were created by Roberto: *Saddam Hussain/threat-pretext*, *George W. Bush/peace-war* referring to the Iraq campaign, *Fidel Castro/tyrrany-freedom*, *Osama bin Laden/dead-alive*. Roberto and Renato cooperated on the word pairs *faith/hate* referring to two motivations behind the conflict in the Gaza strip, *victory/defeat* referring to when Bush was re-elected, *bluff/bomb* referring to North Korea, *suicide/right to die* referring to euthanasia, *democracy/civil war* after the victory of the US forces in Iraq, *heal/sin* referring to stem cell research.

Nagfa

Nagfa stands for Naguib bin Ngadnan and his wife Fadilah bte Abdul Rahim from Singapore. Nagfa's ambigram career started with reflections, inspired by metal/death bands' logos, from where it slowly moved on to simple rotational designs. According to Fa, the secret behind Nag's talent as an ambigram artist is dyslexia and, like the magic behind one of their ambigrams, this secret is two-fold: Nag is dyslexic and is inspired by his 'sexy Dila' (an anagram of Dyslexia). Hundreds of Nagfa's ambigrams can be admired at nagfa.blogspot.com. Nagfa also runs a monthly ambigram challenge. In their ambigram-free time Nag and Fa are Malay-language teachers.

sugar & spice, malayalam, bling bling, firefighter, Bhagavad-Gita, philosopher, home/away, maelstrom, stand by me

home
away

ROBERT MAITLAND

Since 2000 Robert Maitland has been one of the most visible ambigram artists on the web by maintaining one of the largest ambigram websites, www.ambidextrous.quintopia.net; he constantly creates new ambigrams for his online gallery. In creating his ambigrams, Robert tries to be as innovative and original as he possibly can and hardly ever settles for an easy kill. Speaking of killing, don't ever challenge Robert to a duel. His weapons of choice are trebuchets and catapults, which he builds for fun and competition in his ambigram-free time.

Archimedes, trebuchet, T-shirt, eye twisters, eclipse, inevitable, midnight, mediocrity, internet, awesome

Alain Nicolas

Alain Nicolas is the author of the book *Parcelles d'infini* (parcellesdinfini.free.fr) in which he introduces the reader to the wonderful world of Escher-like tessellations. With his tessellations he aims at 'revealing the marvellous worlds which one can give birth to on a simple sheet of paper when one is inspired by the beauty of the natural order and the laws which govern our universe'. Merging the ideas of Escher's tessellations with ambigrams, he has also created many original tessellations with words.

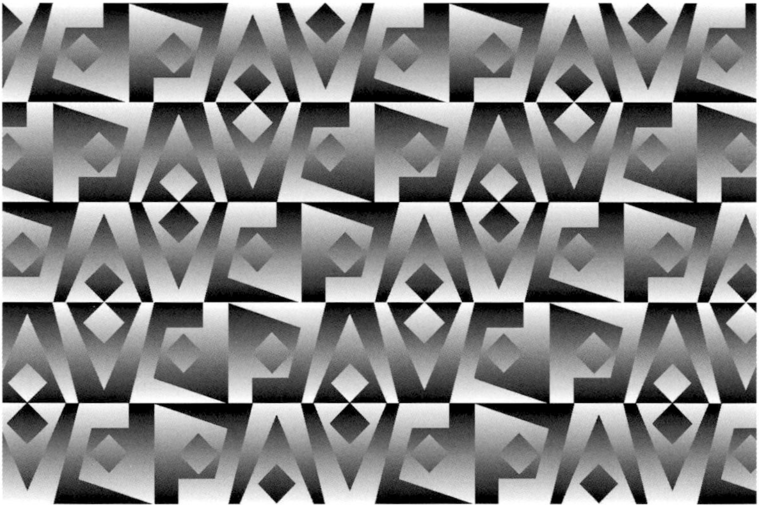

Tessellations with the word *PAVE* and Alain's surname. *PAVE* means tile in French and *pavage* translates to tiling or tessellation. But of course this tessellation also works in English.

NICOLAS
NICOLAS

Hud Nordin aka 01101001

Hud Nordin is a right-brained person doing a left-brained job. Fortunately, he is somewhat ambidextrous. While his software-engineer body goes logically about life in Silicon Valley, the starving artist trapped inside celebrates and creates. Hud tries to bring all of himself together on his website, 01101001.com.

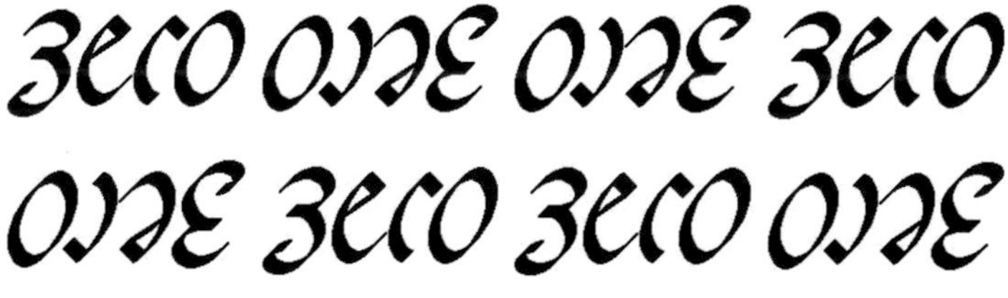

human being, zero one, yahweh, plasma, icon, Escher, Sir Ma'am, Li in black (strength in Chinese) together with *Li* written in white

MARK PALMER

Mark Palmer has a rare passion for letterform that has come to control his life over the past few years. His love for lettering was discovered at a very young age through calligraphy and graffiti-style artwork, but he was always looking for something more. Naturally, ambigrams were the next evolution in his development as a typographer. In the three years since he has discovered the art of ambigrams, he has completed more than three thousand ambigram designs for people all over the world. Though he himself is not a tattoo artist, most of Mark's designs have been permanently inked into the skin of his clients. His design studio, located in Southern California, is called *Wow Tattoos* and can be found on the internet at www.wowtattoos.com.

WOW TATTOOS

Left: the beginnings of two ambigram name alphabets by Mark Palmer: *Abigail*, *Bridget*, *Chelsea*, *Diana*, *Emily*, *Faith* … and *Austin*, *Blake*, *Connor*, *Donovan*, *Edgar*, *Franklin* … and Mark's *Wow Tattoos* logo. This page: his *angel/devil* ambigram in situ.

Tom Banwell

Tom Banwell has always loved words – their history, their etymology, fonts, handwriting and wordplay, such as reading words backwards and looking for other words within them. As a professional mould-maker he thinks upside-down and backwards in three dimensions on a daily basis. As an artist who works in many different mediums, including graphics the combination of his love of words, his love of graphics, and his inclination to think backwards makes ambigrams his perfect pastime. See more of his work at www.lumicast.com.

Patrice Hamel

With one of his ambigram installations (*Répliques*), visual artist Patrice Hamel invites the viewer to appreciate how individual letters combine into an ambigram, to figure out the self-referential nature of the piece of art and to observe how it fits into the surrounding (in situ). Hamel has also created musical spectacles as a director, lighting designer and scenograph. He does research into the senses and the relationship between image and music and is a professor of scenography at the Ecole Nationale Supérieure des Arts et Techniques du Théâtre in Lyon, France. Patrice Hamel has written several books dedicated to texts that have multiple readings. Visit his website for more examples of his ambigrams and information about his other works of art: www.patricehamel.org.

Punya Mishra

Punya Mishra is a professor of educational technology at Michigan State University. He loves looking at the world in weird ways and ambigrams are just one of the many things he likes to play with. You can find his huge ambigram gallery and much more at www.punyamishra.com.

David Moser

In 1988 David Moser met Douglas Hofstadter and Scott Kim, who introduced him to ambigrams. Since he was studying Chinese at the time, he became interested in creating his first bi-scriptal ambigram with Chinese and English. David is a visiting professor in the English Department of the Beijing Foreign Studies University in China.

Kevin Pease

Kevin Pease was introduced to Scott Kim's *Inversions* and Douglas Hofstadter's *Gödel, Escher, Bach* at a young age. For most of his life, ambigrams have been an idle pastime. He is a self-employed graphic designer, scattering his attention among various creative projects including fantasy art, his comic strip *Absurd Notions* (see his website www.absurdnotions.org) and ambigram commissions (see his website cerulean.st/ambigram). He lives in New Jersey.

Brett Gilbert

Unlike many other ambigram pages, Brett J. Gilbert's ambigram website is all about quality and not quantity; see www.ambigrams.co.uk. Plan on spending some quality ambigram time there, as thousands of other people do every month. In his ambigram-free time, Brett works as the Technical Design Manager for a major online retailer in the UK and enjoys playing and designing board games, card games and puzzles.

Paul Agule

Paul Agule has been an independent designer, writer and inventor for several decades in New York City. His fascination with all aspects of design has led him to explore logos, book covers, toys, games, puzzles, packaging and many other areas. He is a graduate of Cooper Union Art School and taught design courses for many years at Pratt Institute and the School of Visual Arts. Paul enjoys the whimsical, and loves what he calls 'unlearning' – in other words, seeing things anew.

E-mail: pagule@att.net

Hop David

Hop David publishes a weekly, small-town newspaper for the community of Ajo, Arizona. While growing up in Arizona, he was surrounded by Native American art, which is rich in geometrical motifs. Later he fell in love with the art of Escher. His work can be seen at www.clowder.net/hop.

J. D. Hillberry

While growing up in Wyoming, J. D. Hillberry began developing his own techniques of blending charcoal and graphite to give a photo-realistic look to his drawings. J. D. uses this monochromatic medium to focus the viewer's attention to the drama of light, shadow and texture without the added influence of colour. Throughout his career, he has tried to push the limits of realistic expression with drawing. After moving to Colorado in 1989, he began experimenting with *trompe l'oeil* drawings. See more examples of his work at www.jdhillberry.com.

Ken Landry

Ken Landry is an artist living in Seattle, Washington, USA, who was inspired by the work of M. C. Escher. He is a retired prosthodontist and builds static models of wooden model sailing ships as his hobby. See more of his work at www.landryart.com.

Jos Leys

There were several reasons why Jos Leys opted for an early retirement after an engineering career in the chemical industry, but one of them was to have more time to dedicate to his passion of creating mathematical art. The quest to produce images that no one has ever seen before is now going stronger than ever. You can admire many more samples of his work at www.josleys.com.

Sandro Del-Prete

Sandro Del-Prete is famous for his highly original illusions. His work has featured in many publications and exhibitions, including two books, *Illusorimem* and *Illusoria*. Find out more about his work at www.del-prete.ch.

Peter Raedschelders

Peter works as a paint-engineer for General Motors in Belgium. His hobbies include art, egyptology, mathematics and making tessellations. His work on tessellations was inspired by Escher's masterpieces. However, he always endeavours to make up new types of tessellations that Escher did not think of himself; see www.ping.be/~praedsch.

Henry Segerman

Henry Segerman is a graduate student in mathematics at Stanford, soon to be a postdoc at the University of Texas. When not researching (in three-dimensional geometry and topology) or teaching, he explores domains restrictive enough to turn the making of art into the solving of puzzles. His work can be seen at his website, www.segerman.org.

Gustave Verbeek

Gustave Verbeek is famous for a series of amazing upside-down cartoons which appeared in the Sunday edition of the *New York Herald* in 1903 and 1904. Every one of the cartoons would start out with six panels which, when turned upside-down, turned into six more different panels.

William E. Wenger

Bill Wenger is a former US intelligence officer, now retired in Tucson, Arizona, where he has finally found time to pursue his interest in graphic arts and, in particular, the work of M. C. Escher. Bill's goal is to produce tilings that are more than simply derivative of Escher's work. Recently he has begun to focus on creating polymorphic figures that periodically tile the plane in more than one way. Examples can be seen on his website at www.miracerros.com/artwork.

SOLUTIONS TO THE PUZZLES

This inkblot spells *inkblot* and John Langdon's inkblot next to it spells *Imagination*.

The whole painting depicts a slave market, whereas the negative space created by the doorway and the figures in the middle also combine into Voltaire's face.

The figures from left to right spell out *Salvador*, and *Dalí* is hidden in the spaces between the objects.

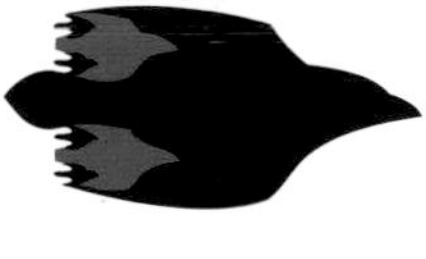

The two elusive birds in Hop David's painting, here highlighted in red.

Two angry faces hiding in the Canadian flag.

Can you see them now by just looking at the flag?

Nine out of ten is quite *often*, isn't it? And *often* is the opposite of *seldom*, just as *in* is the opposite of *out*.

Napoleon is hiding in between the trees.

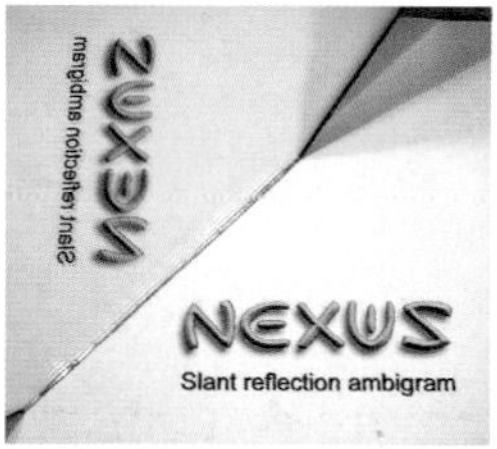

The picture shows how you access the second reading of Tom Banwell's *Nexus* ambigram by using a mirror.

In the mirror image of the Art Car photo the letters on the licence plate appear reversed. This mirror image is exactly what you would see if you looked at this Toyota in your rear-view mirror. By the way, did it ever occur to you that TOYOTA is almost a natural ambigram and palindrome? You can make it into one by adding an *A* in front.

Hint: cover the left halves of all the symbols.

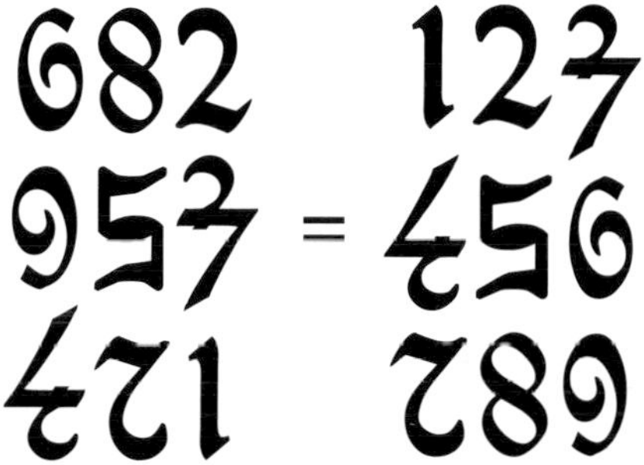

Turn 180 degrees to put the decimals in order.

Sudoku puzzle solution.

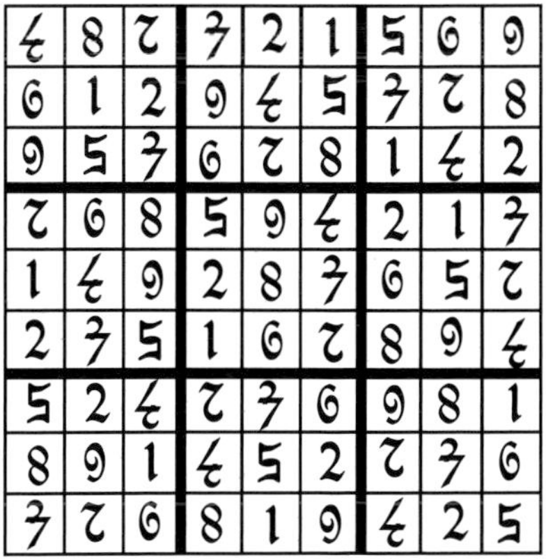

umop ap!sdn

To decode the secret message one of the usual (for this book) actions will work: look at the message in a mirror, turn it upside-down, etc. For added fun, try to imagine the results of these actions before you actually execute them.

The solution of the cryptoambigram is Ben&Alexis. The really hard part is to see that at the end 9=XIS (which is 6=SIX upside-down).

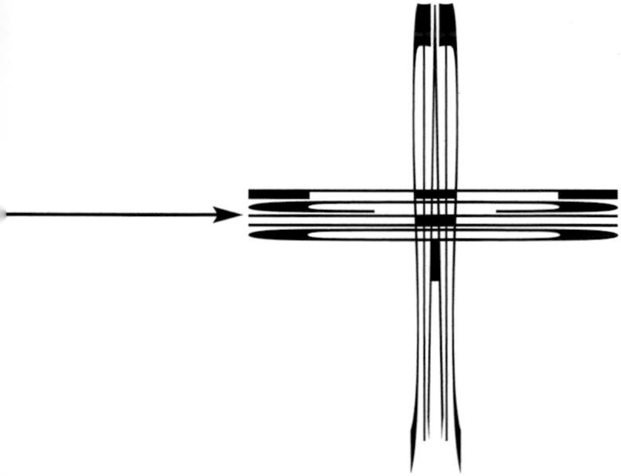

Move one of your eyes close to the page on the left side of the star and look in the direction of the arrow. Viewed like this the horizontal bar turns in the word *echo*. Look at the cross in the same way from the bottom and the vertical bar turns into the word *star*. The design is mirror-symmetric because both *echo* and *star* are written in a mirror-symmetric way.

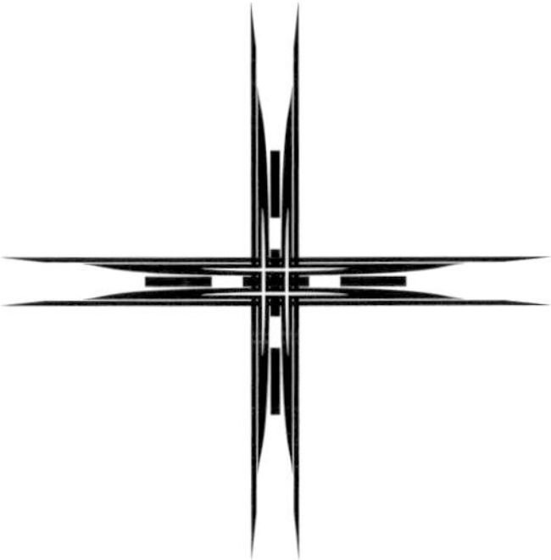

To decipher this cross follow the instructions as above for *Echo Star*. Note that this cross is even nicer than *Echo Star* in that it reads the same, no matter whether you look at it from the right, the left, the top or the bottom: you always see Robert Petrick's *ideal* ambigram.

How many presents?

The number of presents on the 12th day of Christmas would be 13 x 12/2 = 78. For 1,000 days, it would be: 1001 x 1000/2=500,500.

Smiles is the longest word in the English language because there is a mile between its first and last letters. Our ambigram is the longest ambigram because there are two miles between its first and last letters.

CARBON DIOXIDE Often, people's first guess is that this has something to do with the different colours that you used in writing the words. If your victims fail to come up with the right answer, repeat the experiment using the expression ATOM BOMB written from top to bottom. Why does only the second word change? Of course, the solution to this puzzle is that DIOXIDE is a lake-reflection ambigram. If you don't have a wine glass handy, the CARBON/DIOXIDE trick also works if you first give the piece of paper a half-turn and then look at it in a mirror.

Answer to the magic squares problems:

96	11	89	68
88	69	91	16
61	86	18	99
19	98	66	81

The first magic square turns into another magic square when you turn it upside down. Easy.

18	99	86	61
66	81	98	19
91	16	69	88
89	68	11	96

The nine words correspond to two magic squares.

five	twenty-two	eighteen
twenty-eight	fifteen	two
twelve	eight	twenty-five

5	22	18
28	15	2
12	8	25

4	9	8
11	7	3
6	5	10

You get the second magic square by counting the numbers of letters in the words: five has four letters, twenty-two has nine, etc.

The last square is magic in many different ways, four of which are easy to guess: the square is magic the right side up, upside-down, right side up in a mirror, upside-down in a mirror.

8888	1118	1181	8811
1811	8181	8118	1888
8111	1881	1818	8188
8811	8818	8881	1111

1111	1888	8188	1188
8818	8181	1881	1118
8881	8118	1818	1181
1188	1811	8111	8888

1188	1811	8111	8888
8881	8118	1818	1181
8818	8181	1881	1118
1111	1888	8188	1188

8811	8818	8881	1111
8111	1881	1818	8188
1811	8181	8118	1888
8888	1118	1181	8811

All columns, rows and diagonals in all these squares add up to 19,998. In addition, in every one of these magic squares the four corner numbers, the four numbers in the centre, and a few other combinations also all add up to this magical constant. Impressed?

There is more. If you replace all the 8s in the first square by 0s, then you get a magic square of binary numbers. Translate all these binary numbers into decimals and add one to every single one of the numbers and you get back to Dürer's magic square!

The general principle for conjuring up this type of magic square was discovered by Ron Lancester of Hamilton, Ontario.

Solutions to Scott Kim's *Double Talk* puzzles:

mirror, echo, hotshots, fantasy, toy, symmetry, mathematics, myth (it is lying on its side), dance, belief.

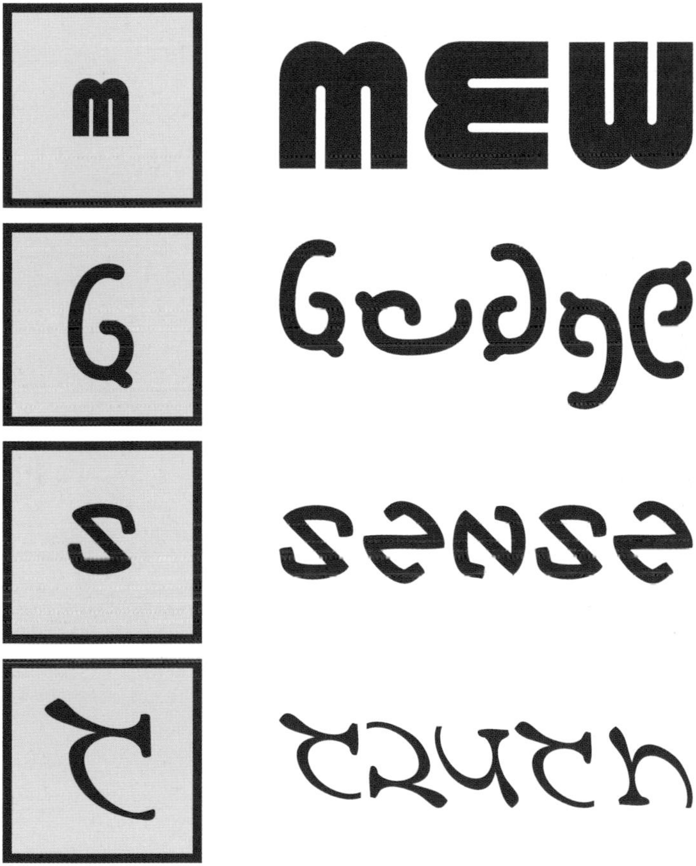

Answers with possible other words that can be formed with the same shape in brackets: mew (be, me, we, bee, ebb, ewe, wee, web), bridge, sense (nee, see, seen, sees, senses, sneeze, sneezes), truth (dud, hut, rut, tut, hurt, thud, tutu, truth).

Recommended Reading

J. Richard Block, *Seeing Double*, Routledge, 2002. Another fantastic book on ambiguous pictures by Richard Block.

J. Richard Block and Harold E. Yuker, *Can You Believe Your Eyes?*, Gardner Press, New York, 1989. One of the best books on optical illusions.

C. C. Bombaugh, *Oddities and Curiosities of Words and Literature*, edited and annotated by Martin Gardner, Dover, New York, 1961. One of the truly legendary works on the curious bypaths of literary recreations.

Michael Donner, *I Love Me, Vol. I: S. Wordrow's Palindrome Encyclopedia*, Algonquin Books, Chapel Hill, 1996. An utterly fantastic collection of palindromes.

Bruno Ernst, *The Magic Mirror of M. C. Escher*, Taschen, 1994. One of the best books about the art of the famous Dutch graphic artist M. C. Escher.

Patrice Hamel, *Répliques*, éditions Al Dante-Théâtre de Roanne, 2000. A collection of Patrice Hamel's ambigram installations.

Patrice Hamel and John Cornu, *Patrice Hamel*, éditions mf, 2006. Another collection of Patrice Hamel's ambigram installations.

Douglas R. Hofstadter, *Metamagical Themas*, Basic Books, 1985. This book contains a chapter on ambigrams with some examples of Douglas Hofstadter's ambigrams.

Douglas R. Hofstadter, *Ambigrammi* (in Italian), Hopefulmonster Editor, Firenze, 1987. A collection of many ambigrams and insightful essays about ambigrams.

Scott Kim, *Inversions: A Catalog of Calligraphic Cartwheels*, W. H. Freeman & Company, 1989. A standard reference and must-have for anybody interested in ambigrams.

John Langdon, *Wordplay: Ambigrams and Reflections on the Art of Ambigrams*, Harcourt Brace Jovanovich, 1992. A new revised and expanded edition was published by Broadway Books in 2005. A standard reference and must-have for anybody interested in ambigrams.

John Langdon, *Ambiguity in Language – John Langdon Paintings 1996–2004*, a catalogue of an exhibition of John Langdon's paintings at the Noyes Museum of Art, available from John Langdon: www.johnlangdon.com.

Dave Maurice, *The Dictionary of Wordplay*, Teachers & Writers Collaborative, New York, 2001. Everything you ever wanted to know about the different ways to play with words – palindromes, anagrams, charades, etc.

Peter Newell, *Topsys & Turvys*, Dover Publications, 1964. A selection of upside-down cartoons from the books: Topsys & Turvys by Peter Newell, Century company, 1894 and Topsys and Turvys – Number 2 by P. S. Newell, Century company, 1902.

Alain Nicolas, *Parcelles d'infini – Promenade au jardin d'Escher*, Belin – Pour La Science. Lots of original tessellations by Alain Nicolas.

Burkard Polster, *Les Ambigrammes – L'art de symétriser les mots*, Editiones Écritextes, 2004. A little book mainly dedicated to mathematical aspects of ambigrams.

Sandro Del-Prete, *Illusorism, Illusorimes, Illusorisms*, Benteli Verlag, Bern, 1981. The first collection of Sandro Del-Prete's original artwork.

Sandro Del-Prete, *Illusoria*, Benteli Verlag, Bern, 1987. The second collection of Sandro Del-Prete's original artwork.

Julian Rothenstein and Mel Gooding, *The Playful Eye*, Redstone Press, 1999. A fantastic collection of very rare illusions.

Ina Saltz, *Body Type*, Abrams Image, 2006. A book about typographical tattoos, including a number of ambigram tattoos.

Gustave Verbeek, *The Incredible Upside-Downs of Gustave Verbeek*, Nostalgia Press, 1976. A collection of twenty-six of Gustave Verbeek's incredible upside-down cartoons.

Acknowledgements

This book would not have been possible without the help of many fellow ambigram and illusion artists who have given me permission to reproduce their work in this book. Many thanks to Paul Agule, Tom Banwell, Hop David, Sandro Del-Prete, Renato Fernandez, Roberto Fernandez, Brett Gilbert, Patrice Hamel, J. D. Hillberry, Douglas R. Hofstadter, Scott Kim, Ken Landry, John Langdon, Jos Leys, Robert Maitland, Punya Mishra, David Moser, Nagfa, Alain Nicolas, Hud Nordin, Mark Palmer, Kevin Pease, Robert Petrick, Peter Raedschelders, Julian Rothenstein, Ina Saltz, Henry Segerman and William E. Wenger.

Among all these artists I am particularly indebted to John Langdon. Without his support over the years this book would not have been possible.

I am grateful to the following companies for letting me reproduce various artworks owned by them: Artists' Market, Norwark, CT, Folkmanis Inc., Gala-Salvador Dalí Foundation, The M. C. Escher Company B. V., Simon & Schuster, Superinteressante magazine, Tenyo Company and Veja magazine.

Thank you also to a few artists who gave me permission to use some of their work which in the end did not make it into the book: Russell Bertolette, Matt Chisholm, Kagi Marketplace. I also very much regret that I was not able to capture Pierre Fourny's fabulous *poésie à 2 mi-mots* animations (alisfr.free.fr) well enough to be able to include some samples in this book. The same is true for Andrew Lipson's and Daniel Shui's Lego models of some of Escher's drawings (www.andrewlipson.com).

Other people who have contributed in various ways to this book coming into existence and whom I would like to thank very much are François Almaleh, Jim Banting, Pam Brooks, Andreas Campomar, Yolanda Del-Prete, Kais Hamzah, Becky Hardie, Gareth Hobbs, Hiroshi Kondo, Alexandre Liverneaux, Marty Ross and Melissa Scannell.

Finally, and most importantly, thank you to my wife Anu for countless suggestions for improvements to the text and my ambigrams.

Pages X (Word/Play), 1 (Wordplay), 3 (Wordplay), 9 (Wordplay), 10 (Starship), 27 (Us), 43 (Relativity, Gravity), 49 (Angels & Demons), 51 (No end/On and on ring that the vortex on this page is based on), 63 (Bridges), 66 (Beware), 73 (Carpe diem), 81 (No limitations), 83 (Burkard Polster), 87 (Choice/Decide), 88 (My metaphysical mirror, front), 89 (My metaphysical mirror, back), 90 (Imagination), 96 (Us), 101 (The persistence of influence), 105 (Years and years), 107 (Love/Hate, Optical illusion), 123 (C'est la guerre), 126 (Survey), 138/139 (True/False ambigram), 140 (Transparent), 141 (Retrospect), 150 (Philosophy/Art & Science, Angels & Demons ambigrams), 159 (cryptoambigram), 193 (Earth/Air/Fire/Water diamond), 194 (Wordplay cover), 195 (Angels & Demons), 221 (The persistence of influence), 222 (Survey), 224 (cryptoambigram) © 2007 John Langdon

Pages 52 (Turtles drawing), 53 (Magician drawings), 218 (Magician drawing) © 2007 Jos Leys

Pages 71 (Volte-Face), 79 (second Fantasy/Reality), 206 (Archimedes, Trebuchet, T-shirt, Eye twisters), 207 (Eclipse, Inevitable, Midnight, Mediocrity, Internet, Awesome) © 2007 Robert Maitland

Pages 99 (Good/Evil), 135 (Links), 215 (Good/Evil) © 2007 Punya Mishra

Pages 110 (China), 111 (Tokyo), 112 (Sea, America), 113 (China, two Chinese mirrors), 215 (China) © 2007 David Moser

Pages 129 (Malayalam), 204 (Sugar & Spice, Malayalam, Bling Bling, Firefighter), 205 (Bhagavadgita, Philosopher, Home/Away, Maelstrom, Stand by me) © 2007 Nagfa (Naguib and Fadilah)

Pages 40 (Escher), 41 (Jour/Nuit), 50 (Plout), 70 (Gentil/Mechant), 71 (the two heads/tiles), 72 (Judo), 208 (Pave), 209 (Nicolas) © 2007 Alain Nicolas

Pages 210 (Human being/Being human, Zero/One, Yahweh), 211 (Plasma, Icon, Escher, Sir/Ma'am, Li) © 2007 Hud Nordin

Pages 79 (first Fantasy/Reality), 152 (Faith, Love and Michele/Gareth ambigrams and photos), 153 (Live/Live and Agape ambigrams and photos), 212 (Abigail, Bridget, Chelsea, Diana, Emily, Faith, Austin, Blake, Connor, Donovan, Edgar, Franklin, Wow Tattoos logo), 213 (Angel/Devil ambigram and photo) © 2007 Mark Palmer

Pages 64 (Wonderland), 74 (Imagine), 90 (Inkblot ambigram), 215 (312) © 2007 Kevin Pease

Pages 9 (Angel), 12 (Ideal), 84/85 (Art/Life), 86 (Ideal), 92 (Evolve ambigram and photo), 161 (the Ideal ambigram that the cross on this page is based on), 200 (Organic, Art/Life), 201 (Magic, Love & Peace, Angel), 225 (the Ideal ambigram that the cross on this page is based on) © 2007 Robert Petrick

Pages 47 (Impossible City drawing), 218 (Butterflies) © 2007 Peter Raedschelders

Pages 68 (Japanese upside-down head), 115 (Japanese upside-down head), 127 (Napoleon), 222 (Napoleon) reprinted with the permission of Julian Rothenstein from *The Playful Eye*.

Pages 150/151 (all photos on these pages) © 2007 Ina Saltz, Angels & Demons tattoo: designer John Langdon; artist, Karl Kegers; photographer, Andrew King; Philosophy/Art&Science tattoo: designer, John Langdon; artist, Steve Andres.

Pages 130 (Dodecahedron), 131 (Dodecahedron tiles and letters), 219 (Dodecahedron) © 2007 Henry Segerman

Page 74/75, Simon & Schuster – 'Ladies of the Lake' reprinted with the permission of Atheneum Books for Young Readers, an imprint of Simon & Schuster children's Publishing Division from IMAGINE A NIGHT paintings by Rob Gonsalves, text by Sarah L. Thomson. Copyright © 2003 Rob Gonsalves and Byron Press Visual Publications, Inc. Text and illustrations copyright © 2003 Rob Gonsalves.

Page 76 (Infinitely many questions) © 2007 Superinteressante magazine, Brazil

Pages 114 (Heavy, Electricity), 115 (Ureshii/Kanasii) © 2007 Tenyo Company (Mr Hiroshi Kondo)

Pages 118 (Bin Laden/Dead or Alive), 202 (Bush/Peace-War, Bin Laden/Dead-Alive, Faith/Hate, Victory/Defeat, Bomb/Bluff), 203 (Saddam Hussain/Threat-Pretext, Fidel Castro/Tyrrany-Freedom, Suicide/Right to die, Democracy/Civil war, Heal/Sin © 2007 Veja magazine, Brazil

Pages 54 (fish tile and tessellation), 55 (fish tessellation), 219 (fish tessellation) © 2007 William E. Wenger

Every effort has been made to trace copyright holders and we apologize in advance for any unintentional omission. We would be pleased to insert the appropriate acknowledgement in any subsequent edition.